Dr. H. KENNETH

Getting Hooked on Memoirs

Preserve and Share
Your Life Experiences
Before They Are Lost

iUniverse, Inc.
Bloomington

Selected comments:

"Your story of Robert Frost's visit to the Wesleyan campus in 1953 is heartwarming and memorable, and it must become part of the Wesleyan Archives." <u>Suzy Taraba</u>, Wesleyan University Archivist

"Love your songs, but it was the memoir of your 1992 Rotary visit to New Zealand that I enjoyed the most." <u>Glenn Estess, Sr.</u>, Past Rotary International President

I read "the Athletics Newsletter with its delightful memoir of spring training in Frederick. I knew I'd like it, and I did." (1/30/09) Thanks for "the delightful account of your phone calls with Kelly and ambidextrous Greg Harris. It's warm and unusual material, very American." (5/07/09) "I loved your piece about the Methodist boy holding a baby for the Pope. It amply justifies my thesis – and yours – that no amount of invention can beat what people actually do; the truth is endlessly surprising and absorbing. The fact that you persevered in tracking down the photographer after 45 years is equally unexpected and gives the story a satisfying credibility." (7/15/09) <u>William Zinsser</u>, Noted Author and Educator

Thanks for the song "My Pre-Game Routine." "I always enjoy taking a look back at my career and remembering all the pre-game rituals." (8/09/06) <u>Cal Ripken, Jr</u>.

1960s Training Camps "were special days with special people, the team, the fans" Balto Colt <u>Raymond Berry</u>

Special words of thanks: Many persons have offered me encouragement as they listened to my memoirs and responded to the stories I shared at memoir workshops and book fairs. The love for memoirs was present at every session. In addition, I especially thank William Zinsser, noted author and educator, for his numerous phone conversations and letters that I highly treasure. Others kind with their words of advice were Suzanna Tamminen, Director of the Wesleyan University Press, and Suzy Taraba, Wesleyan University Archivist. My dear friends Bernice Beard and Dr. Donald Makosky used their literary skills to keep my publication goals on track. Thanks to all!

Front cover: "Fisherboy" by W. C. Jennette is an oil print of an original work by Richard Eichman.

Dr. H. KENNETH SHOOK

Getting Hooked on Memoirs

Preserve and Share
Your Life Experiences
Before They Are Lost

Getting Hooked on Memoirs
Preserve and Share Your Life Experiences Before They Are Lost

iUniverse books may be ordered through booksellers or by contacting:

iUniverse
1663 Liberty Drive
Bloomington, IN 47403
www.iuniverse.com
1-800-Authors (1-800-288-4677)

Because of the dynamic nature of the Internet, any web addresses or links contained in this book may have changed since publication and may no longer be valid. The views expressed in this work are solely those of the author and do not necessarily reflect the views of the publisher, and the publisher hereby disclaims any responsibility for them.

Any people depicted in stock imagery provided by Thinkstock are models, and such images are being used for illustrative purposes only.

Certain stock imagery © Thinkstock.

ISBN: 978-1-4502-9613-7 (sc)
ISBN: 978-1-4502-9614-4 (ebook)
ISBN: 978-1-4502-9615-1 (dj)

Library of Congress Control Number: 2011906642

Printed in the United States of America

iUniverse rev. date: 7/5/2011

Table of Contents

MY GROUND RULES FOR MEMOIR WRITING

It is my opinion that every book or collection of memoirs needs an introductory statement which clearly states the author's ground rules. This approach would correspond to the pre-game routine conducted prior to most athletic events. The umpire or game official calls the team captains together and discusses rules and special conditions that apply to that event. Memoir writers need to do the same thing. I wrote my first memoir in 2003, and prior to putting my words on paper, I had surveyed much of the material written on the topic of memoirs. I admit to you that the term "memoir" means different things to different people, and it seems that each writer is allowed to put his or her own spin on the topic. My thoughts and conclusions were rather well formed when I came in contact with articles and books written by William Zinsser. The writings of this educator and author convinced me that my thoughts on memoir writing were on the right track, and I have often stated that Zinsser's best advice on writing memoirs is to "Think small!"

By the year 2005, my willingness to "think small" had allowed me to produce some seventy memoirs that dealt with a wide array of memorable happenings in my life. At some point, I would follow another of Mr. Zinsser's suggestions. I would spread the memoirs out on the living room rug to study the best ways to arrange them into meaningful categories. When you do begin grouping your memoirs, you'll find it takes a lot of thought, because each memoir has the potential to belong to numerous groups. The year 2005 was also the year that I began conducting sessions on writing and sharing memoirs. In those workshops, I shared my knowledge on the topic as we sought answers to the following basic questions: 1) What is a memoir? 2) Does it have a desired length? 3) Should the details of the writer's experience or happening be true? 4) Could the writer be sharing the experiences of others rather than his own experiences? 5) How does a memoir differ from a research paper? 6) How does it differ from a complete life-history? 7) Should the writing be directed toward a certain audience, such as the writer's own children and grandchildren? 8) Could the topics of memoirs include events of recent weeks or months and not focus solely on events of the distant past? 9) Could writers of memoirs be teenagers rather than senior citizens? 10) Could memoir topics include happenings that many people have experienced and not be limited to "once-in-a-lifetime" experiences?

I view a memoir as an effort on the part of an individual to share a meaningful experience with another person or group. Often the memoir takes the form of a short story with a beginning, middle, and an ending. The middle section would most often describe the memorable event or happening. The beginning would explain why the writer was present and it sets the stage. The ending would point out the results caused by the event and it makes known the impact on the writer or speaker. When possible, the story details should be restricted to a rather narrow span of time which covers the event, and the author's thinking during that time-period could be a vital part of the narrative.

The memoir could be as short as a page or two in length, and photographs and sketches could often enhance the presentation. The event could take place in a few minutes, but it could also be much longer in time. The longer the time-frame, however, the more likely it becomes a life-history rather than classified as a memoir. The memoir event should be the writer's own personal experience, and the details should be true as best the author can recall them. Memoir topics need not be limited to rare events that defy logic and approach the unbelievable, and they should not be research papers. Finally, my memoirs are written to be shared with everyone and not limited in their use to just entertain family members and friends.

My book, *Getting Hooked On Memoirs*, is written with certain goals in mind. I hope to generate in you and others a sincere interest in memoirs and also to motivate everyone to preserve and share their precious life experiences. All of my memoirs are true accounts of my life, exactly as I remember them, and I enjoy sharing the accounts with interested others. My book will offer me an opportunity to share a number of my memoirs with others, but I admit to you that my preference is to relate my life experience orally rather than in writing. Facing the audience and sensing their reactions to my story provides me with the greatest satisfaction, one not gained by publishing a book.

Only a few of my memoirs qualify as once-in-a-lifetime happenings. It is fine to write a memoir about an experience that others have also shared, such as buying penny candy. It need not be a unique happening. The interesting people you describe as having an influence on your life need not be celebrities or winners of a Pulitzer Prize. At times, my memoirs are structured to follow a chronological pattern, but even then, each memoir should have a stand-alone capability. Your memoirs could date back to your childhood and others could focus on events as recent as last week. A Peanuts cartoon had Snoopy The Dog typing memoirs while seated on top of his dog house. Trying to remember old happenings, he wrote "What I remember about last week . . . ."

I am proud to say that I view William Zinsser as a personal friend, and I highly recommend Mr. Zinsser's publications as a great resource for you and any reader of my memoir collection who are motivated to begin the process of preserving life's memorable experiences. Like Mr. Zinsser, I too am an educator, and nothing would please me more than to learn that my memoirs have motivated others to record their special memories, either verbally on tape or in writing. Everyone has stories that deserve to be preserved, and delays in taking action could cause those memories to be lost forever. I hope that you enjoy my memoirs, and I hope that you decide to take that important first step by "thinking small."

Thank you for allowing me to share some of my precious moments with you.

Ken Shook April, 2010

SEVEN KEY STEPS IN MEMOIR WRITING

Where are you on the sequence of steps?
1. First, generate a list of memorable life experiences, and help it to grow in size.
2. Select a few that are most worthy, and type at least two pages about each event.
3. Put completed memoirs aside before polishing them and checking spelling, etc.
4. As your list of topics grows and weeks pass, return to polish some earlier writings.
5. When your polished memoirs reach 40 or more, spread them out on the living room rug, and try to group them into categories.
6. By now, you should be sharing your polished memoirs with others, even groups.

7. When you share your memoirs with groups and you could hear a pin drop, then consider having your memoirs published.

WHEN I WAS YOUNG

The memoirs that follow discuss six events that occurred as I was growing up in Frederick, Maryland, between 1930 and 1947. The events are presented in a chronological order, but all are independent of each other. My Frederick family is pictured below.

In this 1950 Shook family photo, minus brother Charlie, are (right to left): Dad, Mother, sister Cathy, Mom-Mom Burgee, and me. Our small home was on South Market Street, across from the Maryland School for the Deaf.

THE DAYS OF PENNY CANDY, 1935-1941

Historic Frederick, Maryland, was the place of my birth in the year 1930, and the 1930s were seen as the depression years by many of us growing up in these United States. During my "Days of Penny Candy," a period extending from 1935 to 1941, I viewed the few pennies in my pocket as prized possessions. Pennies were spent with care, and those opportunities for me to select from a wide variety of candies that sold for a penny a piece brought me great pleasure.

From age five to age eleven, a list of my choices of penny candies included: *B-B Bat Suckers, Boston Baked Beans, Bubble Gum & Baseball Cards, Candy Corn, Caramel Bull's Eyes, Chocolate Babies, Circus Peanuts (Banana), Gold Coins, Green Spearmint Leaves, Horehound Drops, Indian Pumpkin Seeds, Jaw-Breakers, Jelly Beans, Jujubees, Lady Fingers, Licorice: Black Cigarettes, Licorice: Square Plugs, Licorice: Black Straps, Licorice: Red Strings, Malted Milk Balls, Mary Janes, Orange Slices, Paper Strips & Dots, Red Hot Dollars, Root-Beer Barrels, Tootsie Rolls, Turkish Taffy, Watermelon Strips, Wax Lips & Wax Bottles.*

In addition to these items, we were also able to purchase the following brands of chewing gum products: Beechnut, Black Jack, Clove, Dentyne, Juicy Fruit, Teaberry, and Wrigley's Spearmint. If five-cent candies were added to the list, we could also consider: Baby Ruth, Bit-O-Honey, Butterfinger, Clark Bar, Hershey Bar, Mars Bar, Milky Way, Oh Henry, Powerhouse, Snickers, etc. Although not a candy, Smith Brothers Black Cough Drops was a popular licorice product, and I ate the cough drops like candy.

I never thought of myself as living in poverty, but our

household was certainly a low-income family in the 1930s. As children, my brother and I had very little money to spend, and it was a treat anytime Charlie and I had the opportunity to attend a movie or to buy candy. My father grew up on a farm and his formal education was limited. He never held a high paying job. My mother on the other hand was a graduate of Hood College, but she chose to be a stay-at-home mother. It was fortunate that Mom loved to cook and sew, so we always had tasty home-cooked meals and homemade clothing. Some of our shirts were made from attractive feed sacks, and many of my pants were hand-me-downs made of corduroy material, material that never seemed to wear out. Brother Charlie was two years older than I, so he avoided much of the hand-me-down experience. When he and I were old enough to work outside of the home, we always held jobs to provide our spending money. Like many other youngsters, our first jobs were delivering newspapers, and we never had to share part of our income with our parents to meet household expenses. Nevertheless, we were always aware that our Christmas lists were at best "wish lists, not reality lists." It was well known that our mother liked Russell Stover chocolates, and a small box of mixed chocolates was often my gift to her. She made candies like fudge and peanut brittle at home, and candy apples on occasion.

Our home in Frederick during my penny candy days was located at 213 East Patrick Street, and this was just two doors from the US Post Office. The large pavement in front of the Post Office was an ideal place to play games and roller skate, and persons entering the building for stamps would sometimes pass through a hockey game in progress. Slightly more than a block away from my Patrick

Street home was my elementary school on Church Street. The school was close enough that my brother and I could race from home to the school while the City Town Clock was striking nine o'clock. We left on the first strike and were in our classroom seats before the ninth strike of the clock. The Church Street School had candy sales on certain occasions, and the hard taffy made in the shape of circular discs was my favorite of those penny candies, especially if the taffy contained nuts. A poorly dressed man often appeared at the front of the elementary school selling foot-long pretzels, and those mustard covered pretzels cost a penny. Unsanitary, but good.

When I entered the fifth grade, I changed schools, now attending the North Market Street School, which was some seven blocks from my Patrick Street home. It was now necessary to ride my bike to avoid being late for school. I fondly recall that I was selected to be a school patrolman for that year, and I was proud to wear the white belt and AAA badge. I helped students to cross at the busy Fifth Street intersection, and every two weeks, a movie pass was given to each patrolman. Movies cost about ten cents in those days, so passes were happily received. When I used the free pass, I could plan to spend five cents on candy, and the five cents paid for a bag of taffies, a bag about the size of a half-loaf of bread. I can recall eating candy during the entire movie, and a sizable portion would remain to be taken home. At this time in my life, I also acquired a taste for lemon drops, and a bag of drops was often found in my pocket. A few friends began calling me "The Lemon Drop Kid." Thankfully, the name did not stick. In Frederick, the best stores for candy were the "Five & Ten" stores. Of these, Woolworth's was the largest store, and Newbery's was the smallest. Drug stores were also reasonable candy suppliers, but the candy sold at the movie theaters was a bit overpriced. Their boxes of candy cost at least a nickel.

My favorite memory of buying penny candy would have to be my purchases made while spending summers on my grandfather's farm. "Park Hall," shown here, was his farmhouse, and it was part of Civil War history.

During that war, troops would stop at Park Hall to rest before proceeding on to battle at Gettysburg. Horseshoe marks were visible on the floor of the front hallway, indicating that military horses were ridden into the house, perhaps to be concealed from soldiers of the opposing army. The farm was located just east of the Frederick city limits, quite close to the Frederick Fair Grounds. I loved summers at the farm, and Pop-Pop would pay me to sucker rows of corn and pick up rocks in the fields. My grandfather wanted me to save the pennies he gave me, and I admit, using Pop-Pop's antique clown bank was a lot of fun. The idea was to place your coin into the clown's hand, and he would then throw the coin into his mouth, never to be seen again. Some of my pennies did follow that route, but a few coins would find their way to the purchase of penny candies. A restaurant next to the farm just happened to sell penny candy, and my favorite item was a licorice block on a stick called a Jungle Bat. This penny candy required at least a half hour to eat, making it a great bargain. I believe it was my grandfather who told me that licorice was found in the ancient tombs of Egypt, so I was impressed that my love for licorice was shared by ancient Egyptian rulers who lived 5000 years earlier.

You'll notice that I never indicated a craving for chocolate candy, but back in the 1930s I found that chocolate candies often melted in the bag or all over my hands. This made quite a mess, and I wanted to avoid the problem. When I did have chocolate candy, like a Milky Way bar, I often stored it in the ice box and ate it while it was cold. This way the chocolate would melt in my mouth and not on my hands. If these words remind you of another well known chocolate product, let me state that the popular M&Ms candies made their appearance in 1941, a bit late to be included as part of my "Days of Penny Candy" experience.

For the Shook family, Easter was another of the special times to give and receive candy treats. Mother always received a box of her favorite Russell Stover chocolates, and Charlie and I were often allowed to make our choices before anyone else sampled the sweets. Each of us received Easter baskets, and the baskets always overflowed with candy, hard-boiled eggs, and fruit. Hard-boiled eggs were sometimes hidden about the house for us to find, and of course, community Easter egg hunts were held at Frederick's Baker Park. The reason we stopped hiding hard-boiled eggs at home was because some well-hidden eggs were not found for months, not until a smell led us to the forgotten hiding place. Chocolate eggs were better than the hard-boiled variety, but real eggs were needed to hold egg-pecking contests. As you may recall, the winning hard-boiled egg was the one that cracked the shell of the other egg. Some jokers always tried to substitute raw eggs into the egg-pecking contests.

A popular time in elementary school was Valentine's Day, and I recall the sharing of cards and candy hearts. The cards were placed in a box on the teacher's desk, and it was nice to receive cards from classmates. I believe that I made some of the cards that I gave to others, since most store-bought cards were beyond my budget. The small candy hearts were a lot of fun to give and to receive, because they had printed messages on them, adding joy to penny-candy days.

SUMMERS ON MY GRANDFATHER'S FARM

In the year 2001, I sent a letter to my brother pointing out that he and I had very different opinions about our grandfather, Professor Amon Burgee. I, for one, was placing him on a pedestal and saw him as my greatest role model in life. Many people in the Frederick, Maryland, community agreed with my assessment, and a monument was erected in Pop-Pop's honor at his grave site in the Mount Olivet Cemetery. Charlie seemed to be tearing down my idol, and the letter that follows was my strong response to my brother.

Dear Charlie,   September 4, 2001

As I was reading your account of life on Pop-Pop's farm, I realized that your experiences did not parallel mine. I enjoyed riding the plow horses and eating the raw vegetables (carrots, turnips, and potatoes), and the availability of fruit was a big plus. The grapes were plentiful, as were the apples. The morning breakfast at the large kitchen table was a highlight for me, and to this day, starting the day with a good breakfast is a must. I enjoyed helping Pop-Pop when people drove down the lane to buy corn. He took great care to inspect each ear of corn that was purchased, and a dozen ears usually counted out to thirteen for some reason. Pop-Pop would talk to customers and never rush them off.

Pop-Pop enjoyed working in the field, but when he vanished from sight, I always suspected that an afternoon baseball game was being broadcast on the radio. Night baseball was not yet the norm, so summer afternoon games were a regular occurrence. Since I loved ball as much as he did, I would join him. He would suggest that we needed to return to work after a few minutes, but seldom did we turn off the radio. The static could change our minds, especially when the broadcast originated from some distant city. My favorite announcer was Arch McDonald of the Washington Senators. He would often hit a gong to designate the number of bases reached on a particular hit. The homer was exciting when the gong sounded four times. One of the few times Pop-Pop showed his temper to me was in a crucial part of the game when radio static made it impossible to hear the broadcast. I thought he was going to toss the radio out of the house.

Pop-Pop's failure to pay me the full amount of money for my work in the cornfield was the only time that I ever thought him to be unfair. I thought it was my experience alone until I read your similar account. I do not recall being a part of a group, so your memoir does not match mine. My story must have been shared with you, because I was very upset over the happening. I had recorded my daily work accomplishments in a small book, and I proudly showed the book to Pop-Pop at the end of the week. I was saving money for some goal, and every penny was committed. He looked at my book and seemed to be impressed by the record keeping and the workload. None-the-less, he said the money I claimed was too much for a boy of my age. I told him he was unfair, and he never tried to change my opinion. The amount he handed me may have been half of that which I expected. After that I curtailed my work in the field suckering corn and recording the daily results.

On the farm, Mom-Mom loved to have me comb and brush her long hair, and I enjoyed doing it. Since I was small, I often stood on a box behind her chair to be able to reach her hair. I also remember that Mom-Mom's sewing basket was always near at hand, and numerous times she would need to repair a rip in my clothing. She always used thimbles when sewing, but seldom would she use scissors. Generally she would break the thread with her teeth, and I thought this was quite funny to watch. Aunt Grace lived on the farm in these early years, and she took me to the Frederick Opera House to see movies on many Monday evenings. It seems that a short feature on those evenings was "Death Valley Days," and Aunt Grace did not want to miss a single episode of the series. She told others that the movie going was solely for my amusement.

I was happy that the Frederick Fair Grounds was in walking distance of Pop-Pop's farm, as was VanAcore's Restaurant, one of my sources of penny candy. Getting candy to eat on the farm was a real treat, and my favorite was a penny sucker called a "Jungle Bat." It cost a penny and could take about an hour to eat, if my memory is correct. It was fun to play with the coin banks at Pop-Pop's, especially the clown bank, and sometimes I tried my hand at drawing farm scenes. Wood supplies were delivered to the farm for some unknown purpose, and the delivery included some pieces in the shape of rectangular solids. On some of these blocks, I used to sketch farm scenes; my best sketch was a drawing of the old barn. Could that block still be in the back of some dresser drawer? Could someone have burned that wooden block, not realizing its full value? Milking time on the farm was another fun occasion for me and my cousins. We could hear Uncle Ray singing to the cows as he milked them. I cannot imagine any other life than farm life for Uncle Ray, and I doubt that he ever felt forced into the "farmer" role or felt mistreated by Pop-Pop as you seem to suggest.

My summer work in the fields was not easy, but I actually enjoyed the change from jobs that I held in Frederick during school months. Drinking water out of buckets in the field was an experience. Bugs and debris usually found floating on the water's surface had to be brushed aside before taking a drink. Regardless, the water tasted just great on a hot day. It is true that most of our farm duties seemed to be picking up rocks and suckering corn, but not all of our time was devoted to back-breaking work. In Pop-Pop's study, I sometimes looked over school textbooks that he had used in his high school teaching, and I was impressed with Pop-Pop's notations in the margins. He always seemed to be exploring thoughts that the authors failed to include. One of Pop-Pop's school papers was a debate extolling the role of women in our society.

When Pop-Pop spoke to persons visiting the farm, he often thought for a while before responding to their questions. Rather than give hasty remarks, his care made his comments more significant. If he told a student he would fail in life, I suggest that this may have been the perfect case for justifying the use of "reverse psychology." Such a method does not always work as a motivating instrument, Charlie, but apparently it did succeed in the case you depicted.

Pop-Pop loved the earth, and he seemed to enjoy his role and his many successes in life. He was certainly proud of the affection and honors that came his way, but I do not recall any boastful actions on his part. He did not go in for show, and he often dressed in well-worn clothes that were held together with safety pins. I sometimes wished he would be more conscious of his appearance when visitors came to buy corn. I, for one, feel that Pop-Pop deserved the praise and accolades heaped upon him, and I have never questioned his love of family, church, and community.

Many other memories of the farm still are fresh in my mind, but I will close. The account of the black snake that our bare feet nearly touched on that run up the lane will have to wait for another time and place.

Younger brother,
Ken   (Copy to our sister, Cathy)

Added note: I was always fascinated by the comments that Pop-Pop placed in the margins of text books that he used when he taught all of the high school subjects. I also found his handwritten copy of A DEBATE: WHO HAS THE GREATER INFLUENCE? MAN OR WOMAN? He wrote it in 1911 to share with his students as a possible closing argument in a debate. It goes as follows:

Need I point out that almost every idea of right, of intelligence, and of Christianity the average man gets, he gets from woman, and yet two gentlemen on the other side have the audacity to stand up here and claim Man has exercised more influence than Woman. What if Man has fought battles and overturned governments? Do you mean to tell me that God in his goodness looks with favor on such a horrible sight as Mexico and Turkey has just experienced? The Bible does say there shall be wars and rumors of wars, but nowhere does it say there should be wars. About the only claim to great-ness that Man has is his record in battle. How

PROF. AMON BURGER

he loves to be called General, Captain, and Colonel. He forgets there is an unseen battlefield in every human breast, where two opposing forces meet, but where they seldom rest. Tis the conquest of the heart God delights in, and there, Woman excels.

What would this country be without homes, and what would homes be without mothers? The absence of a father is scarcely noticed, but when mother is gone, all is gone! The same is true of churches. Tis true under present conditions that preachers are largely men, but tis likewise true, the congregation is largely women, while our saloons, jails, and penitentiaries are filled with men. Can it be that saloons, jails, and penitentiaries are more influential than churches? I can't believe it, honorable Judges, and I am sure that you don't.

Love, says Henry Drummond, is the greatest power in the world, and next to the love of God, the greatest influence in the world is the love of mother, wife, and sweethearts. What is man without the love of his mother, his wife, or his sweetheart? Our opponents would have you believe that a woman is simply a tombstone, whose only duty in life is to weep at the grave of some self-inflated, self-praised man. Instead of all men being demi-Gods, honorable Judges, a large number could more appropriately be called demi-

Johns. But what is the use of my talking longer? The sinking stars and the waning moon would invite you to sleep ere I could begin to tell you of the silent and most wonderful influence of Women.

Man is much like a skyrocket. He explodes and starts off with a whiz, but returns in the form of gas, while Woman is like the beautiful sun in the sky, that extracts water from the seas, and restores it in the dews and the rain, for the blessings of all mankind. I regret I must close, but my time has expired. When the gentleman who is to follow has made his pathetic appeal, for tis most pathetic to plead a losing cause, I say when he has pronounced the benediction, extend to the offender your sympathy and congratulations, then do the manly and square thing, vote unanimously for that last, best, and by far most attractive of all God's creation, lovely, bewitching, attractive Woman.

NEWSPAPER DELIVERY BOYS WORE KNICKERS

A Rotarian friend, Robin Saul, happened to be the Editor of the local newspaper, The Carroll County Times, and he explained that youngsters stopped delivering newspapers in the 1980s for mainly two reasons. First, the cost of preparing copies and printing the papers had reached the point that only adults could be allowed to deliver the valuable product. What had once sold for pennies was now sold for dollars. The second factor seemed to be the move away from afternoon deliveries to mainly early morning newspaper deliveries. Youth were no longer an available labor source when most newspaper deliveries were made between four and six o'clock in the morning. My reaction to the Editor's words was one of sadness, as I reflected on the benefits that came to me in the late 1930s when I delivered newspapers and worn knickers.

I was a newspaper delivery boy between 1939 and 1944 in Frederick, Maryland, and that was my first employment experience. True, I had performed odd jobs to earn spending money in earlier years, but those tasks lacked regularity and seldom did they stress personal responsibility. My first paper routes were close to home, and my customers were often people I knew quite well. The rather small bag of newspapers generally hung from my shoulder as I walked the route, but on occasion, I would use my small wagon to help in the delivery. As my routes got larger and moved further away from home, a bicycle with a large basket became a necessity. I no longer walked to the front porches for a delivery, so papers were folded in a way that they could be tossed from the sidewalks with a high degree of accuracy. Papers landing in bushes or on roof tops had to be retrieved, otherwise, customers would lodge complaints with the newspaper office. In rainy weather, plastic bags were used to cover the papers, and the delivery time on those days was much longer than usual. My father may have driven me around my paper route on a few of the bad-weather days, but no such occasions come to mind. If extra papers remained after completing my route, I naturally worried that some customers had been missed and that complaints would follow the next day.

Although newspaper editor Robin Saul said youth were not available to deliver papers in the early morning hours of the 1980s, I do remember delivering papers in the early morning hours of the 1940s. One experience that I never forgot was the time that I collided with another bike rider, and both of us ended up seated on the street staring at each other. It must have been about 4 AM, and I expect we were both tired and half-asleep. The collision woke us up, and without saying a word to each other, he retrieved his belongings and I picked up my newspapers, and we each rode off in opposite directions. I later counted the papers in my bag, and to my surprise, the count was correct. Apparently, I had not missed any of my customers on the first half of my paper route, and this had been accomplished while not fully awake. I received no complaints the next day.

My bike collision incident took place during the summer months, at which time I actually held three jobs. Two jobs were morning newspaper routes that required about three hours to complete, and following those tasks, I worked in a small donut shop for another three hours. Every week or two, I needed to collect money from most of my newspaper customers, and I recall that such collections took place on weekends. Some customers made this task easy, but some never seemed to be at home when I rapped on their doors. My love for math problems and working with numbers was evident even at this early point in my life, so I actually enjoyed collecting payments from customers. Many of the other newspaper boys disliked this responsibility, and some made calculation errors that cost them their jobs and angered their subscribers.

During my newspaper delivery years, I often wore knickers that extended from the waist to just below the knees. Pants of this length were perfect for bicycle riders. Longer pants could possibly get caught in the bicycle's chain or caught on the pedals. Since I was two years younger than my brother, Charlie, I naturally got his "hand-me-downs." His sneakers never came to me, because shoes had a short life span, but knickers never seemed to wear out in those days. This was especially true of knickers made of corduroy material. These pants were indestructible! To prove my point, I remember the time that I had an accident while playing at the Braddock Height's Amusement Park. Our family often visited this park located just outside of Frederick, and its huge sliding board allowed 6 or 7 people to slide down at the same time, seated side by side. The park was on a mountain top, so its gravel covered roads were steep, and on one occasion I ran a bit too fast for my own good. My feet could not keep up with the upper part of my body, and I took a beautiful swan dive, landing hard on the gravel surface. Hands and knees were cut and bleeding but the knickers I was wearing showed no damage at all. Later that night, when I undressed for bed, I realized that my right knee had a hole in it large enough to lay a finger in, and the knee required many stitches. The corduroy knickers on the other hand showed no damage. As I said, they are indestructible!

After speaking with my Rotarian friend about the demise of newspaper delivery boys in the 1980s, I had occasion to drive to the Billingslea Medical Center in Westminster, Maryland. The morning newspaper was lying on the sidewalk in front of the building, so I did my good deed of the day and delivered the paper to the reception desk in the lobby. The young receptionist on duty had a confused look on her face when I said: "Collecting for the paper!" I laughed as I pointed out to her that she was too young to remember how boys, and occasionally girls, delivered the daily newspapers in the 1970s and 1980s, and how once every two weeks they knocked on doors to say "Collecting for the paper!"

I'm told that many famous people shared my experience as a paperboy, including such notables as: Harry S. Truman, Dwight D. Eisenhower, Norman Vincent Peale, Walt Disney, Bob Hope, Bing Crosby, John Wayne, Martin Luther King, and Tom Brokaw. Sadly, the paperboy experience will no longer be the first job had by youth, and it has apparently been replaced by working at McDonalds and Berger King.

THE FIFTH GRADE'S SCHOOL SAFTY PATROL

Now that the upper 70s refers to my age and not my golf score, I admit that I am flattered when a cashier at a restaurant asks if I am a senior citizen. As a rule, I avoid such questions by ordering off of the senior menu. My closest friends include men and women of all ages, but again, I have to admit that many are of retirement age. When we talk about the "good old days," we are not referring just to the past twenty or thirty years. As mentioned in another memoir, people in my age group regret that boys and girls will no longer be able to say that their first employment was delivering newspapers, because youth lost access to these jobs in the mid-1980s. Likewise, I assumed that boys and girls would no longer have the joy of wearing AAA badges and assisting their classmates in crossing at street corners. Fearful of lawsuits, the thinking in the 21st Century apparently demands that adults act as crossing guards for all students walking to and from school.

Pat Amass, a Westminster resident, shared a photograph of her East End Elementary School patrol group which was taken in the late 1940s. The photo, on the next page, shows that the number of girls in that patrol slightly exceeded the number of boys. Pat is third from the left in the second row. I mentioned to Pat that I was chosen to serve as a Safety Patrol member when I entered the fifth grade in the early 1940s, and wearing the white belt and AAA badge was a very proud moment for me. My regular assignment was the busy intersection located at the corner of 5th Street and Market Street in Frederick, Maryland, just one block away from the North Market Street Elementary School. There, I occupied my position for the half hour prior to school and the half hour

East End Elementary Safety Patrol - 1946 photo

immediately following school. Once every two weeks, each of us was issued a movie pass, and that was indeed a special treat in those days. The movie pass was honored at the smallest of the three Frederick movie houses, and for this reason, I mainly used my pass to see a Saturday cowboy movie. Since the movie was free, I was able to purchase a large bag of candy, more candy than I could possible consume on one visit to the theater.

Many of my senior-age friends added their own memories of school safety patrol days, and one retired gent still had his AAA badge from those early days. A few recalled being in safety patrol parades that marched down Pennsylvania Avenue in Washington, DC. None of them had received movie passes for their patrol duties, because all of their patrol groups had been located in schools in Westminster, Maryland, and not located in my home town of Frederick. One former Carroll County School Superintendent thought that the use of students on school patrols had ceased in the mid-1980s, and another, who was unsure of a date, gave me the name of a school official who could answer the question about the demise of school patrolmen. The knowledgeable contact proved to be a person currently employed at the Maryland State Department of Education in Baltimore.

My phone call to the State Department was taken by Bill Cappe, and I stated that a group of us wondered about the date that students ceased to serve as members of school safety patrols in Maryland. We had judged the date to be in the mid-1980s. It took him about a minute to control his laughter, and he then explained his reaction to my inquiry. At the very moment I called him, he was dialing the Superintendent of Frederick County Schools to secure the number of students planning to attend the School Patrol Day at the Baltimore Oriole baseball game that Saturday. For the 50th consecutive year, the Orioles were holding an event to honor school safety patrol members, and school patrol boys and girls were coming to Baltimore from all parts of Maryland to join in the celebration. Bill Cappe said that his desk was filled with forms requesting the use of the 10,000 student tickets available for the Saturday baseball game, and our conversation caused him to conclude that none of those requests had been received from the schools of Carroll County.

My senior citizen group was pleased to learn that the school safety patrol program was still alive and well, at least in most of the other counties of Maryland, and we wished that Carroll County schools had not been an exception to the rule. Members of my Westminster group expressed the unbiased opinion that "the good old days" which allowed students to serve on school safety patrols had ended too soon in Carroll County and deserved to be reactivated in the near future.

* * * * *

SANTA MISSED OUR CHIMNEY IN 1940

While our parents were worried about the fighting and bloodshed in Europe in 1940, we children had other things on our minds. Our "war effort" was limited to wrapping tinfoil from discarded cigarette packs into balls and collecting wagonloads of old newspapers. Typical of youth, we were thinking about playing "Cowboys and Indians" and attending Saturday morning matinees. We were using rubber from old inner tubes to make slingshots, while some lucky boys were shooting Red Rider BB Guns. Our school desks in 1940 had pencil slots and inkwells. On the radio, we listened to The Shadow, My Friend Irma, and Lux Radio Theatre, and in the funny papers, we enjoyed Little Orphan Annie, Maggie & Jigs, Mutt & Jeff, and Captain Marvel. We liked parades, band concerts in the park, and watermelon festivals, and we laughed when dogs chased cars down the street. We sometimes purchased a 5-cent Popsicle using the pennies we received for returned soda bottles or pennies we earned by pulling weeds in the back yard. We enjoyed car rides, and the frequent tire blowouts were not our concern. Nor were we worried that penny postal cards and regular 3-cent stamps might increase in price. We were, however, worried that Santa Claus and our parents might overlook our Christmas list, or that Santa might possibly deliver our Christmas gifts, by mistake, to some other less deserving youngsters.

In December of 1940, my brother, Charlie, and I did everything right, trying to insure that each of our Christmas wishes would become a reality. During the 1930s, times were hard for our family, so in those years we wished for very little, and that is exactly what we got. In hard times,

24

our mother might sew us a home-made shirt, the material coming from colorful feed bags, and our father might build us a toy wagon or a sand box. The 1940 Christmas was going to be different. We knew it! The family was a bit better off, so Charlie and I both asked for and expected to receive bicycles with attached baskets. These bikes would allow us to provide all of our own spending money by delivering newspapers in the Frederick community. Also, we now needed bikes to ride to our schools that were many blocks away from our home, and no buses or other transportation were available.

Charlie and I were singers, and the words of the song written by Coots & Gillespie were familiar to us. We not only sang the lyrics, but we believed every word of each verse to be true, just to be on the safe side. Yes, *Santa Claus Is Coming To Town!*" we thought, and getting on his list required our best behavior. The lyrics clearly indicated that Santa had a list, and that he was checking it twice and also watching our behavior.

My brother was two years older than I, but in 1940, I sometimes acted as if I were the older brother. I was thinking that Charlie and I had a list, and our parents had a list, and Santa had a list. *What if the three lists did not agree?* Charlie and I were also concerned that Santa might confuse one house with another, and he might possibly go down the wrong chimney with our gifts. After all, in our eyes, Santa's body was showing some age, perhaps even reaching the age of forty or beyond. It was hard to speak to Santa face-to-face in 1940, so a letter was mailed to Santa's home at the North Pole. I attached a 3-cent stamp, wondering if it was enough postage.

As stated earlier, prior to 1940, Charlie and I wrote

Christmas lists that were quite short. Our expectations were never great, recognizing that our parents were not able to buy gifts with large price tags. As an example, on one Christmas, my single request was for a pilot cap, and it brought me enjoyment for many months. Pretending to be a pilot was great fun, and I could even turn the goggles to protect my eyes while I was in flight. Mom was a college graduate, but she opted to stay at home while Charlie and I were young, so she did not add to the family income. On the other hand, she was a great cook, and she enjoyed housework. Dad had a limited amount of schooling, but he was a good car mechanic, and he loved police work. He never did receive a large annual income, but all things considered, we managed pretty well as a family.

Charlie and I held a variety of jobs in the Frederick community, and we provided nearly all of our own spending money, particularly during the high school years. We even purchased most of our own clothes, especially during the years that we were employed at the Abe Ellen Haberdashery. This men's clothing store was located in the famous Francis Scott Key Hotel in Frederick, and it was while working there that I purchased my first quality suit, a tan gabardine suit by Hart, Schaffner & Marx that would never wear out.

The big day arrived. On that Christmas morning in December of 1940, Charlie and I rushed downstairs at the break of dawn, and no bikes were found under the tree. *How could this be? What mistakes had we made? Did the three lists not match? Had Santa given our bikes to others?* Charlie and I were in pain, but we bravely hid our feelings, playing with our other toys. The morning dragged on, and after lunch, the neighbors invited us over to see their tree. Mom, Dad, Charlie, and I walked next door.

The neighbors were Bessie and Sadie Hahn, two elderly sisters. In 1940, our home address was 213 East Patrick Street, and the address of Bessie and Sadie Hahn was 211 East Patrick Street. Charlie and I thought of the Hahn sisters as being quite old, at least sixty years of age or older. We were stunned to see two new bicycles under their tree, and the bikes were exactly the styles that Charlie and I had requested on our Christmas lists. When the adults began laughing at us in the Hahn's living room, we knew that the bikes were for us, and that Santa had indeed entered the wrong chimney to deliver our new bikes. Within minutes, Charlie and I were outside riding our bikes, and in our happiness, we were almost willing to forgive Santa and our parents for the mishap that had occurred on that Christmas morning in December of 1940.

JOCK DIXON WAS LIKE A YOUNGER BROTHER

Jock Dixon is a name that few people will recall, but for several years, Jock was perhaps my closest friend. His full name was James Russell Dixon, but I knew him only as "Jock." Those years were 1943-1946, my freshman, sophomore, and junior years at Frederick High School. How he got the name "Jock" is a mystery to me, because he never was a super athlete as the name Jock might imply. I do not recall how he and I first met, but he just always seemed to be at my side, like a loyal puppy dog. Some common activities could have brought us together, but my major interests were baseball, football, singing, and mathematics, and Jock shared none of these interests. At Frederick High, (see photo)

we shared the same homeroom and some classes. His small physical stature limited him to the sport of basketball, playing at the JV squad level, never varsity.

For as long as I knew Jock Dixon, he weighed no more than 125 pounds, and his maximum height may have reached 5'7" at best. I often worried that he would get hurt playing sports, and even at basketball, the ball appeared to be too large for him to handle. At age five or six, I too was a frail child, and some relatives doubted if I would survive. I had difficulty breathing, and some said that I was pigeon-chested, a description I very much disliked. The removal of my tonsils and adenoids at age six changed all of that, and at the age of thirteen, I entered high school in 1943 as a 5'11" youngster weighing about 190 pounds, no longer a weakling.

When Jock and I were together, I often felt like his big brother and protector. Jock and I were assigned to the same homeroom in high school, and after school, we often visited the local Frederick YMCA on Church Street. Like a matching pair, he and I rode bikes together, and neither of us had much money to spend. We both earned our own spending money, and we carried our lunches to school in brown paper bags. My mother liked to sew, so my clothes were always neat and clean, even if they were hand-me-downs. My knickers were usually previously-worn items handed down from my brother Charlie, who was older by two years.

Jock Dixon never seemed to wear new clothes, and his red and gray coat sweater was always buttoned from bottom to top, giving me the impression that he was chilly at all times. The lack of money meant that Jock and I never went to the movies together, never dated girls, and rarely joined others going to restaurants, dance halls, or bowling alleys. To the best of my knowledge, Jock never visited me in my home, and I do not recall ever visiting his home. Why this was true I have no idea. I can only surmise that Jock was an only child, or, he may have had a sister or two. I continue to believe that I was the nearest thing he had to a brother, and for this reason, my decisions became his decisions. Whatever I decided as a course of action, he inevitably followed the same path. The memorable exception to this behavior pattern took place on an evening in 1946.

One evening in 1946, Jock and I were seated on the steps of the local YMCA. We had completed our basketball play in the gym, and we even took time to play a few games of pool before departing the building. My next move was to ride my bike home, because I knew that several hours of school assignments were waiting for me. A group of classmates stopped their car in front of the YMCA steps, and Jock and I were invited to join them in going to a type of night spot located somewhere along the Baltimore pike. My lack of interest in going to what sounded like a beer hall and my lack of money to spend made my decision an easy one, and I said *Thanks, but no thanks!* As expected, Jock echoed my remarks, and the car departed. A few minutes later, the car reappeared, and we were again extended the same invitation for a joy ride. I refused for a second time, but on this occasion, Jock surprised me when he said he would join those in the car. As he entered the front seat of the car, I was viewing Jock's action as that of a defiant younger brother, telling me he was capable of making his own decisions. The car departed before Jock could change his mind, and that was the last time I saw my friend alive.

It took days for all of the details of the car accident to become known, but the entire high school faculty, staff, and student body were in a state of shock. The speeding car had apparently left the highway and had collided with a piece of road construction equipment parked over-night on the side of the road. The driver of the car and those passengers in the back seat had survived with serious injuries, but the front seat passenger had been killed instantly. Jock had been seated in that front seat, and his body was thrown through the front window of the car, causing his death. For weeks following the tragedy, I often found myself looking behind me, as if expecting to see the friend who was no longer by my side.

My Frederick High School Yearbook of 1947 contained photos of those classmates who died prior to graduation, and Jock's picture was among that small group. Many graduates of 1947 might find it hard to remember Jock Dixon, but some would remember the fellow who had once been my best friend. Many might not remember the often-worn red and gray sweater that Jock was wearing in the Yearbook photo, the sweater that was buttoned from the bottom to the top for extra warmth. Jock and his sweater will always be part of my fond memories of high school days in Frederick, MD.

HIGHER EDUCATION
LEARNING EXPERIENCES

After attending Frederick High School in Frederick, Maryland, I continued on for a year of post-graduate study at the Charlotte Hall Military Academy in 1947. I was still located in Maryland, but this was my first time away from home, and dormitory life was a new experience. College life began in September of 1948, when I enrolled in Western Maryland College. From 1952-1954, a generous fellowship grant made it possible for me to attend Wesleyan University in Middletown, Connecticut. In later years, I concluded my higher education experience at the University of Maryland, receiving a PhD degree in 1968, but learning continued after that.

Since I view the first year of college to be the critical year in any student's adjustment to campus life, I selected a memoir that relates to the importance of college roommates and dorm life when living on campus. The second memoir took place at Wesleyan University, and it tells of my memorable evening with poet Robert Frost in 1953. I think you will enjoy my two selections.

THE IMPORTANCE OF COLLEGE ROOMMATES

When people reflect on the important events and happenings in their lives, it is my opinion that most of those experiences will mainly focus on personal relationships,

relationships dealing with a limited number of individuals, possibly as few as one or two people. As an example, when I led a Group Study Exchange Team to New Zealand in 1992, our six-member team was greatly impressed by the beautiful country, but what each of us listed as our fondest memory of the trip was meeting the people, the Rotary families who opened their homes and hearts to us, becoming our lifelong friends. Another example would be my college dormitory life from 1948-1952. During those years on the campus of Western Maryland College, I was a resident student and was housed in Hering Hall, a corner of an older structure called Old Main. I lived in this unattractive dormitory for all of my undergraduate years, but it was my group of roommates during those four years that made my dorm life a positive experience and not a negative one. Saying it in another way, bricks and mortar are insignificant when compared to the importance of contacts with college classmates and college faculty members. For me, older buildings covered with ivy could be more beautiful and memorable than newer and more expensive structures.

When I entered Western Maryland College in September of 1948, some administrator assigned me to live with three other freshmen in a two-room unit of Hering Hall. I had no choice in the matter, but we adjusted to the crowded situation. A quick decision on our part arranged the two double bunks in one of the rooms, and the four desks were placed in the second room. The thinking was that bright lights used at our desks for late night study should not interfere with those attempting to sleep. Perhaps my roommates knew that I often did my best studying between five and eight o'clock in the morning.

I also remember that our study room windows did not look out in the direction of the neighboring women's dormitory, a safeguard against another type of distraction. My roommates that year were Stan Bowlsby, Jack Loper, and Jan Ports, and our academic majors were expected to be: Biology, English, Mathematics, and Philosophy. We got along quite well, and no one sought new roommates at mid-year.

In my sophomore year, my brother and I decided to share a dorm room, and the decision was a good one. Charlie was starting his senior year, if my memory serves me correctly, and it was good to spend additional time with him. He and I had belonged to the same fraternity, The Black & Whites, and we both sang in the College Choir, but other than that, our paths on the small campus seldom seemed to cross. For a while, we both held campus jobs in the college dining hall, but in his senior year, Charlie worked in the office of the Dean of Men. I remember that our parents benefited by Charlie and I sharing a dorm room. There was only one phone in the third floor hallway of our dorm, so our parents' phone calls had a better chance of catching at least one of us in our room. Laundry and food packages would sometimes be mailed to us from home, and one dorm location for the two of us simplified this process. I don't remember if we imported a small refrigerator from home, but I do recall that during cold weather months, people outside the dorm could see jugs of cider resting on our third-floor window sill.

For my final two years at Western Maryland College, Donald Makosky was my roommate, and this great fellow became one of my very best friends. Don and I shared many interests and activities. Both of us loved sports, music, and religious activities, and we were in the same fraternity for three years. Don's father was Dr. John Makosky, Dean of the Faculty, and his home was about four blocks from the campus. I greatly benefited from Don's decision to live on campus his final two years of college and his willingness to be my roommate. Of course, he did receive some kidding on those occasions when he decided to take the long four-block trip home for a weekend visit. Don's description of me in the 1952 WMC Yearbook included three statements that I still remember: 1) Ken often calls out to me in the dorm room, asking: "Don, what is the correct spelling of this word?" 2) When Ken sings, he always sings to convey a message; and, 3) Ken's religious beliefs are granite firm!

Dormitory life was an enjoyable learning experience for me, and having the right roommates was the blessing that made that possible. I can honestly say that my focus was on roommates and other close friends, and not on the old building in which we were housed. Phones, showers, and bathroom facilities were not provided in any of the dorm rooms, but we learned to adjust to the use of one hallway phone and the use of showers and bathroom facilities that were shared by everyone on that floor. The Western Maryland College women's dorms did have elevators, but none were found in the dorms occupied by male students. While I had comfortable relationships

College Roommates

Don

Jack

Stan

with my roommates and key faculty members in the 1948-1952 school years, I acknowledge with regret that some WMC students did not, and I wish that had not been the case. I suspect that in some of those situations a transfer to another college was seen as the only option open to these students.

The Rest of the Story: An observation that became known to me only after the passage of many years was the fact that my roommates at Western Maryland were

Ken & Charlie

truly unique in terms of their later academic achievements. Including myself, there were a total of six of us in that WMC group, and everyone in the group graduated from WMC, and all in the group satisfactorily completed additional graduate study. One member attended seminary before entering the ministry, and the other five members received PhD degrees. In an age when many students starting college fail to complete their undergraduate studies, I am proud of the academic success of my 1948-1952 Western Maryland College roommates, and I feel honored to have been a member of that group.

Note: Don, Stan, and Jack are shown above as pictured in our 1952 Western Maryland College yearbook, *The Aloha*. My brother, Charlie, testing my arm strength in one of the photos, was a 1950 WMC graduate.

MY EVENING WITH ROBERT FROST IN 1953

The evening I met Robert Frost was in 1953, and he was a guest speaker at Wesleyan University in Middletown, Connecticut. He spoke in the Chapel that evening, and every seat was occupied long before the poet's arrival. It could be described as a standing-room-only event, and many persons were turned away at the door. I recall that I entered by a back door and sat in the choir loft to gain a closer view of Mr. Frost. The loft was where I usually sat as a member of the Chapel Choir, and my thoughts were wandering to a recent concert we performed with the female chorus of Radcliffe College. Since Wesleyan University was a male institution at this time in its history and Radcliffe College was female, the two great schools frequently combined singing voices to perform concerts. My thoughts suddenly returned to the crowded Chapel as the lights dimmed, and the guest of honor entered the hall.

The lighting was poor, and Mr. Frost found it difficult to read his prepared notes. I felt sorry for the elderly gentleman, and I concluded that the evening would not be the inspirational experience everyone anticipated. Mr. Frost was 79 years of age at the time of this visit to the Wesleyan campus, but his appearance suggested an age in the eighties. His best moments were limited to those few times when he left the prepared script and spoke from memory. After the program, I walked a few blocks to my campus residence, the Weeks House, a former residence of Connecticut Governor Frank B. Weeks. This lovely dwelling was now owned by Wesleyan University, and it was designated to be the headquarters for a special

Masters Degree Program. Twelve of us were selected in 1952 for the first year of this Master of Arts in Teaching Program, and a portion of the group shared the Weeks House as a campus residence. The Weeks House had the comforts of a college president's residence, and the library was my favorite room. On that evening, the Weeks library was filled with twelve to fifteen MAT Program students and administrators, and we were discussing Mr. Frost's performance in the Chapel.

The Weeks House, Wesleyan University

Imagine our surprise and shock that evening when Robert Frost walked into the Weeks House library to join us! I offered him my comfortable seat and positioned myself on the floor, leaning against the left arm of his chair. His left leg was actually pressed against my right arm, and I had no desire to avoid the contact. He spoke about his recent travels, and then he noticed that I held a small volume of his poems in my hands. He asked to use the book, and for the next hour, he read from the book of poems. He answered questions about his life and his poetry, and he obviously enjoyed the experience. Unlike his earlier image at the Chapel program, Frost now appeared to be energetic and even youthful. He was a delight, and the room was alive with his wit and wisdom. It was one of the great moments of my life. He asked me for a pen, and he autographed my little book before he left the library that night. As pictured below, the small $1.25 Modern Library Books publication, *The Poems of Robert Frost*, was the book he signed that evening, and it continues to be one of my prized possessions.

THE POEMS OF ROBERT FROST

With an Introductory Essay

"THE CONSTANT SYMBOL"

by the Author

A MODERN LIBRARY BOOK

Robert Frost
Wesleyan 1953

MY MILITARY SERVICE AND TRAVELS

My young age caused me to miss service duty during World War II, but the local Draft Board made sure that I served my two-year obligation. I was allowed to attend Wesleyan University on a two-year graduate fellowship, and the Maryland Draft Board even looked the other way when I taught mathematics in Madison High School, NJ, in academic year 1955-1956. That kindness ended in July of 1956. The first two memoirs in this category relate to my Fort Monmouth, NJ, experiences.

The final two memoirs describe travel events that qualify as "trips-of-a-lifetime." Rotary provided the funds for the New Zealand trip, and the Egypt trip was also reasonable in cost because my daughter was a travel agent at the time. Daughter Jennette also arranged a two-week tour of Turkey, and the tour of Turkey is a memoir waiting to be written.

I maintain that all US citizens should fulfill a two-year service obligation, and everyone should have a daughter who is a travel agent.

THE RED BANK CHURCH, MY SECOND HOME

Following World War II, many young men in the United States faced a military service obligation of two years. Perhaps they had been too young to serve during the war years. Draft boards continued to call persons into the service, and it was hard to predict just when the call would occur. Married men with children could possibly avoid the service, but most could not avoid it. Such service obligations could be delayed by college enrollment and or by employment in certain critical occupations. Military pay was low, and soldiers with families faced the greatest financial difficulties. Some family housing was available on most military bases, and the PX was a place to purchase inexpensive food and supplies. Single soldiers had most of their basic needs provided (food, housing, clothing, medical services, etc.), but civilian clothing, off-base expenses, and retirement savings were often a concern.

For a number of reasons, it was important that all servicemen spend some time off of the military base. Exposure to civilian life gave a balance to one's existence, and being off base was a way to avoid being found when extra military duties needed to be delegated to those soldiers with free time. It was possible to hide out in the base library during one's free time, but all knew that staying in the company barracks was an unwise decision. The barracks would be the first spot surveyed for persons to be assigned extra duties. When hit by extra military duties or when working in the computer labs, I wore fatigues (without a gas mask). When caught to march in a post parade, helmet, orange scarf, and spit-shined boots were also part of my military

dress (see above). My time spent off post allowed me to appear in civilian dress. Playing for the Fort Monmouth baseball team and singing in a quartet (above) that competed in the All-Army Talent Competition were other ways that I avoided being assigned some of the extra military duties.

My Research & Development Company at Ft. Monmouth, NJ, needs some explanation at this point. Everyone assigned to this unique military group had a graduate college degree, a Masters or Doctorate degree. We were brought there to work in the Signal Corp computer labs, and each day, buses transported us to the labs which were some ten miles from the base. At the labs, our bosses were civilians, but on base we were bossed by "regular-army" sergeants and by officers who were often graduates of ROTC programs. As you might guess, my group assigned to work in the labs wanted that duty to be the top priority while the bosses on base (especially the regular army sergeants) wanted parades, barrack inspections, physical fitness, and KP duty to be the top priority. The conflict lasted for the entire two year period that I was stationed at Fort Monmouth.

My life was greatly enhanced by the Red Bank Methodist Church (shown above). It was just fifteen minutes away from Fort Monmouth. It was a perfect church for my needs, and during my two years in the service, it became my home-away-from-home. The Red Bank Methodist Church had an outstanding music program headed by organist John Ferris, and it had an inspirational minister in Reverend Roger Squire. There were many young families and young single people my own age, and social programs seemed to occur weekly. I became a regular soloist in all choir productions, and I sang the lead in two musicals, *Down In The Valley* and *The Telephone* by Menotti. I taught a Sunday school class and directed several religious plays. Bowling was popular in that part of New Jersey, so I became a bowler as well. Many of the young people in this church have remained my life-long friends, and for me, no other church has proven the equal of the Red Bank Methodist Church.

Organist and Choir Director John Ferris and Reverend Roger Squire were two of the remarkable people I met at the Red Bank Methodist Church. John Ferris deserved the accolades I have given him. He devoted tremendous time and energy to his church music, and several years after my departure from Red Bank, he was called to Harvard University to be Head Organist and Choirmaster, a position he then held for three decades.

Roger Squire was minister at the church for all of my two years, and he was a humble man. His true talent was a dedication to serving others, and an aura of love seemed to surround him. It was easy to worship in his presence, and I could sense that the entire Red Bank congregation worshiped him. I was in his home on many occasions, and he directed all of our conversations toward hearing about my life and my future plans. He was reluctant to talk about himself. You only heard about Roger Squire's life from others in the church.

Once Reverend Squire stopped in the middle of a Sunday morning sermon, and he prayed a special prayer for a particular church family, the Stout family. He then returned to his sermon text and completed the service. He said only that it was something he felt compelled to do. Word came later that day that a train wreck had occurred in Connecticut that Sunday morning at the precise time that Reverend Squire issued his special prayer. The Stout family of the Red Bank Methodist Church had been on that train. Mrs. Stout had the most serious injuries that morning, but she fully recovered, and later, she returned to sing in the church choir. She and I often sang duets. Roger Squire was a humble man and a holy man, and his friendship has truly been a blessing in my life.

MY WHIRLWIND TOUR OF EUROPE IN 1957

The month was April in the year 1957, and I was about to embark on my first major tour of countries outside of the United States, and that tour would allow me to visit England and numerous other European countries. Some months earlier, I had requested a 46-day leave from the US Signal Corps, and that military leave had been granted. During a training program for the R & D Company at Fort Monmouth, New Jersey, I had heard a lecturer suggest that servicemen could obtain free flights on military aircraft to distant parts of the world. He then recommended that those of us in the audience with available leave time should use such leave time to travel overseas. I may have been the only person in that audience who followed the lecturer's advice. Dressed in my military uniform, waiting for an empty seat in any plane that was headed toward Europe, I stood at the railing of the airport at Fort Dix in New Jersey, hoping that my name would be called over the loud speaker. After no more than a half hour wait, my name was called, and a plane departing for Burtonwood, England, had an open seat. I accepted the call and quickly boarded the four-propeller aircraft.

As I took my seat on the aircraft, it suddenly occurred to me that other than a car trip to Quebec, Canada, I had never been outside of the USA, and I had never had a flight in a plane. This flight to England was to require a refueling in the Azores, wherever that was, and the total flight was to take some seventeen hours. The plane took off, and in a matter of minutes, it had soared above the clouds. My eyes were glued on the clouds below me, and I imagined myself bouncing on them as if jumping up and down on a giant bed. The clouds looked like cotton balls. The sun shining on the white fluffy surface was a spectacular sight, adding to the thrill of my first flight in an airplane.

Landing and departing the Azores was also a thrill, because the fog actually made it impossible to see your hand in front of your face. How in the world could any pilot land a plane and then take off under such weather conditions? I took the opportunity to stretch my legs, but quickly I returned to my seat since there was nothing to see on the outside of the plane. Hours later, we landed in Burtonwood, England, and fair weather greeted us. My main mode of travel would now be by train, since trains were both speedy and economical in 1957.

At the time of my trip to Europe, I was a single person with limited resources, so I planned to seek rooms in private homes rather than reside in hotels. My military uniform would be worn only to gain entry to a military PX to buy film and other necessities. At all other times, I planned to wear "wash and wear" civilian clothing, thus avoiding cleaning bills. Snacks would be carried in my camera bag, curbing my appetite and holding down meal costs, and it would take years for the smell of cheese to leave that camera bag. Prior to my trip, many friends in New Jersey were eager to help me in planning a strategy for the trip, and they often suggested places for me to visit and people for me to contact. As an example, a red haired London girl, who happened to be related to my friends in New Jersey, agreed to meet me in London. She served as my tour guide, and we concluded the most pleasant day with a dinner and a concert at Covent Gardens. An Argus C3 camera joined me on the trip, and hundreds of photographs would be taken, but the film would not be processed until I arrived back in the United States. My camera had been repaired just weeks before departing New Jersey, and there had been no time to give it a test run. I suppose this indicates poor planning on my part, but the gods smiled on me that day, and all photos developed beautifully.

My first destination was Edinburgh, Scotland, arriving by train, and I checked into a room near the station and began a walking tour of the city. It held my attention for several days, with the old castle and the shops on Princes Street, and then I took a bus ride to Loch Lomond and Ben Lomond. This side trip was very worthwhile. Not only did I see the beautiful scenery, but I also ran into an art teacher, John Lewis. He was from Birmingham. We became close friends, and his impact on my life is covered in another memoir. John made sketches of Loch Lomond while I photographed the quiet solitude. In saying farewell, John invited me to visit him at his home in Birmingham for a steak dinner. Leaving Loch Lomond, my train then headed south, stopping in York and then on to London.

My four days in London included a Sunday, and on that day I sought to have a recommended boat ride up and down the Thames River. I understood that such river tours were popular with American tourists, and the boats departed from a spot near the Parliament Building and Big Ben. Arriving in my light colored raincoat, with my camera hanging around my neck, I found what looked like a ticket booth, and I joined the rather long line waiting to board. The booth never opened to sell tickets, but soon, passengers were directed to board the boat. For more than an hour, we journeyed up and down the Thames, and I moved freely about the boat, taking photos and enjoying the available refreshments. When we returned to the original starting point, passengers departed the boat and began walking away in all directions. I stopped one of the passengers, and asked why no one had attempted to sell me a ticket for the tour. Stretching himself to a fully erect posture, this Londoner seemed to look down his nose at me when he said: "This was a private party on tour, and it was not open to the general public or to American tourists." …. Ouch!

Before leaving England for Paris, I enjoyed a visit to Shakespeare's Stratford on Avon, followed by a dinner with John Lewis in Birmingham. My final stop was to see the White Cliffs of Dover and visit Norwich. One of my older brothers, Herman, had served in the US Air Force during World War II, and he had been stationed in the Norwich area. In fact, he met a girl there, and she became his war bride. I saw the English pub that my brother visited, and I met some of my sister-in-law's relatives who were still living in the Norwich area.

Paris was to be a three-day visit on my tour schedule, perhaps too short a time to see all of the sights that I had listed on my agenda. Europeans as a rule were friendly toward me and toward America, but in France, the French sometimes resented the fact that many Americans could not speak their language. The 1957 Paris prices were high compared to the rest of Europe, but the Eiffel Tower, the Arch of Triumph, the Cathedral of Notre Dame, and the Louvre Museum's Mona Lisa were attractions that outweighed any of my financial concerns. The train's next stops for me were Brussels and Amsterdam. I loved Amsterdam with its side trip to Volendam and Markham. Sheer luck placed me in this area at the height of the tulip season, and the fields of flowers were breathtaking to behold. I took a photograph of a painter at his easel, attempting to capture on canvas the fields of colorful flowers. He must have known that his task was an impossible one. In 1957 Amsterdam, parked cars were known to drift into the canals, and the bike riders were seen everywhere. Rembrandt's paintings, Anne Frank's home, and Amsterdam's inexpensive food made it hard to leave, but Copenhagen beckoned me to the land of Hans Christian Andersen where the Little Mermaid waited.

The Little Mermaid welcomed me and other visitors to the charm and friendly atmosphere of Copenhagen, and a short bus ride to the north delivered me to the summer palace of the royal family. The much-loved leader of Denmark in 1957 was King Frederick, and he had been ruler during the Nazi take-over of his country in WW II. While I stood in front of his summer palace, a slender man came out of the left side of the building and as he passed me he extended a pleasant greeting of "Good morning!" He continued walking across the street to a car parked there, and being alone, he then started the engine and began to drive away. A gentleman, perhaps a Dane, approached me from the rear, and asked if I realized who had just spoken to me, and I said that I had no idea. He said that my greeter was in fact King Frederick, and that he often drives about Denmark without an escort. I had no time to adjust my camera, but I captured on film a blurred image of King Frederick waving his hand as he drove away from his summer palace.

The train ride south from Denmark took me through Germany, and I was surprised how many WW II battle scars still remained in the urban centers. Bombed buildings were still visible in 1957, as if to remind every- one of the evils of war. After a brief stop in Bremerhaven, I proceeded by train to Frankfort. On this particular train ride through Germany, a humorous incident occurred. I had placed two suitcases on the overhead rack of my compartment, and a train inspector entered and asked to see the suitcase contents. Others in the compartment were not subjected to this type of inspection, so I assumed he was showing his dislike for American tourists. Since one of my cases was totally empty, carried only to accommodate future purchases in Europe, I naturally pulled down the suitcase with contents. The inspector would have none of this, and he insisted on seeing the second case. Not able to speak German, I did my best to explain the situation, and finally I brought down the empty case and opened it. His face became blood red in color, and he stomped out of the compartment. Later he returned to say in broken English:

"Big joke! Big joke!" All in the compartment waited for him to leave before we broke out in laughter.

Switzerland had scenic beauty everywhere, and Bern and Geneva provided me with a good sample of Swiss life. While there, I purchased clocks, watches, and wood carvings at reasonable prices, and all fit nicely into my empty suitcase. The air in Bern was crisp and clear, and the word "pollution" was not needed in the Swiss language. The train next stopped in Nice, and during the one-day stay, I toured the famous casinos and I watched the bikini clad bathers on the rock-covered beaches. I was shocked to see beaches with little if any sand. Following the coastline south and then turning east, the train's next destination was Rome. At this point in my tour of Europe, I must admit that I was beginning to tire a bit. Perhaps my 46-day whirlwind trip had been too vast an undertaking. This thought was quickly dispelled when I recalled that Rome, Florence, Venice, and Salzburg were just ahead, helping me to gain a new sense of excitement about the last leg of my 46-day trip.

Seeing the Coliseum and the Vatican Sistine Chapel were clearly the highlights of my stay in Rome, and standing in St. Peters Square, perhaps the most famous square in the world, was impressive. No special services were being held in the Sistine Chapel during my visit, but I did drink in the beauty of Michelangelo's painting of The Creation on the ceiling of the chapel. After a while, the numerous memorable sights of Rome actually caused me to reach a saturation point, and I could no longer separate fact from fiction. The feeling was akin to the high degree of humidity felt just prior to a rainstorm. I actually departed Rome a day earlier than planned, making a hasty departure for

Florence and its less hectic atmosphere. Before leaving Rome, I did have a photographic session with the Pope Pius XII, and that happening is best described in a separate memoir.

For me, Florence, Italy, can best be summed up in the name "David." Upon seeing this masterpiece by Michelangelo, I concluded that I had just seen the greatest work of art the world had ever known. Nothing could match its grandeur. This one statue alone makes any visit to Florence a worthwhile venture. I loved my short stay in this city and wanted to return some day. Venice, my next stop, also had its charm, but I happened to see the city in rainy weather. Under such wet conditions, the quaint canals of Venice reminded me of smelly back alleys and not at all a pleasant tourist attraction. The next stop was Salzburg, Austria, the city of Mozart and known for its beautiful Alpine setting. It deserved a week, but after two days, the train was leaving for Paris and my flight home. We did stop briefly in Oberammergau, where the famous "passion plays" had been performed since the 1600s. The location was impressive. I practiced my stage voice to empty seats.

My trip of a lifetime came to a close with the flight from Paris to the United States. I was tired, but looked forward to sharing my stories and many photographs with those at home. I was now a more experienced traveler, and I had no doubt that the 1957 tour of Europe would remain one of the great happenings in my life. I also realized that the 46-day experience was only possible because of a requirement in the 1950s in the United States that men fulfill a two-year military service obligation. For me, that requirement was truly a blessing.

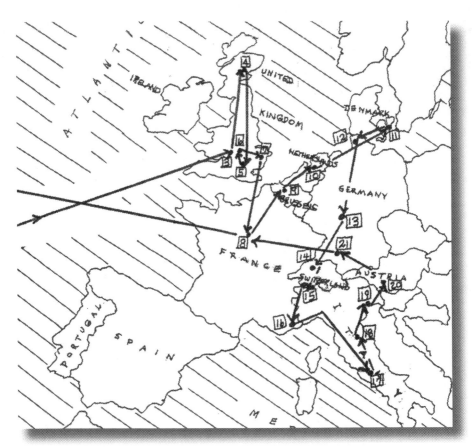

Hand Drawn Diagram of My 46-Day European Tour

<u>By the numbers</u>: 3) Burtonwood Air Force Base 4) Edinburgh 5) London 6) Stratford on Avon & Birmingham 7) Norwich & White Cliffs of Dover 8) Paris 9) Brussels 10) Netherlands & Amsterdam 11) Copenhagen 12) Bremerhaven 13) Frankford 14) Bern 15) Geneva 16) Nice 17) Rome 18) Florence 19) Venice 20) Salzburg 21) Oberammergau 8) Paris & the flight back to the USA

McGuire Air Force Base departure on a 17 hour flight

Ken in Scotland   **David in Florence**

MY ROTARY TRIP TO NEW ZEALAND IN 1992

One of the motivations for joining a service organization is the personal desire of the individual to give something back to the local community and to the world. Individuals who have been successful in a career and have attained a certain comfort level in life often want to share their blessings with those who have been less fortunate in life. "Service to others" must be the focus of "service organizations," and such groups have an unwritten rule that their members should not be the beneficiaries of the financial contributions made to service clubs for their worthy club projects. One of the best-known and most-respected service organizations in the world has been Rotary International, started in 1905.

In 1992, I was proud to call myself a Rotarian, and at that point, I had been a member of the Westminster Rotary Club for 32 years. It was understood that joining a club only made you a club member and not a Rotarian. To become a true Rotarian, one needed to demonstrate years of commitment and service to the ideals of the Rotary International organization. Only then could one expect to earn the title of "Rotarian." One task that helped me to justify holding the title of "Rotarian" was my role as Team Leader of a Group Study Exchange Team (GSE) that went to New Zealand in 1992.

Group Study Exchange became a program of the Rotary Foundation in 1965, and nearly 500 teams travel annually to other parts of the world, visiting a Rotary District for about five weeks. Since Rotary International is composed of over 500 districts, the Foundation pairs up districts each year for the exchange. Our Maryland district, for example, might send a team this year to a district in India, and the following year we might exchange teams with a district in Norway. I was selected from a group of fifteen Rotarian applicants to be the GSE Team Leader in 1992 for our Rotary District, District 7620. After my selection for the Team Leader role, non-Rotarians were then interviewed to fill five positions as Team Members. The team trained for about three months, preparing for the trip, and then the six of us were ready to begin our glorious five-week experience in the North Island of New Zealand. The costs of the program were lowered somewhat by arranging for the team to stay in the homes of Rotarians, and all other expenses, except air travel, were covered by Rotary clubs in the host District. The Rotary Foundation paid for the air travel of all GSE teams.

My GSE team members seated around me in the photo below were (from my right and clockwise) attorney Beth Golden, insurance/politics management Michael Baker, construction architect Dennis Pabst, landscape architect Rhonda Martin, and account executive Pamela Baratta. We flew to California and then on to Hawaii for a one-day rest stop. The entire flight from Baltimore to New Zealand seemed to need a break in the middle, and team members enjoyed some time on the beach. I decided to attend a Rotary meeting, and that club awarded a prize to the Rotarian traveling the longest distance to that meeting. I felt that I surely would win, and I was shocked to learn that the winner of the prize was a Rotarian from New Zealand. Imagine my surprise to learn that my GSE team had not yet reached the mid-point of our flight to New Zealand.

New Zealand is a land that extends from 33 degrees to 53 degrees S. latitude. It is very long and very narrow, consisting mainly of a North Island and a South Island. Most of the North Island sees little snow, but the South Island has snow covered mountains and deep fjords. We first landed in Aukland, and then flew in a smaller aircraft to the southern part of the North Island. Wellington occupies this southern tip of the North Island, and it is the Capital of New Zealand.

Our visiting GSE Team would spend most of our visit in the lower portion of the North Island, the location of our host, District 9940. I told our hosts that the New Zealand map was fine, but I was sorry to see that their world maps were flawed. They laughed when I offered to send them copies of world maps that correctly placed North and South America in the center portion of the page, not on the right edge as depicted on their flawed maps. I also pointed out that there was a bit of confusion in the countries "down under" about the seasons of the year. March, April, and May are of course spring months in the US, but they were fall months for us while in New Zealand and Australia.

The host, Rotary District 9940, made plans for us to sample most of the culture of the region in five weeks. We saw numerous sheep and deer farms. We also visited the famous Victoria University and the Parliament Building in Wellington. We walked the beaches and rowed the rivers. We sang our songs at Rotary meetings, and we danced the war dances with the Maori people. We met the American Ambassador to New Zealand, and we chatted with school children and political figures, but most of all, we ate and ate and ate. Everyone on our team must have gained some weight. I remember that lamb was the dish most frequently served to our team, but a fish and chips meal was always my favorite. A typical breakfast consisted of bacon, eggs, and toast, unless I chose cold cereal and fruit that morning. Many afternoons we took a break from the travel schedule to have tea and scones.

Vocational days were part of the Rotary agenda, and that allowed us to share ideas about our careers and life goals. Toward the close of our visit, we took part in their local District 9940 Conference, and a farewell party was arranged in our honor. Some eyes were damp that day, and we knew that the Rotarians, especially members of the host families, were our friends for life. We flew from Wellington to Auckland, and then we journeyed to Sydney, Australia. Being in that part of the world, we wanted to add one week to see a small part of Australia before flying back to the United States. In the photo, I'm holding a koala in a zoo near beautiful Sydney. My daughter, a travel agent, said that our memorable trip as "ambassadors of good will" could not be duplicated for her clients at any price. We truly lived the "once in a lifetime" experience, and Rotary International made it possible.

I close this account with a few comments about the people of New Zealand. You will never find friendlier people in your travels, at home or abroad. They are truly outdoor people, and they enjoy nature and flower gardens. I feel they are a patriotic people, but they are not ones to "wave the flag," as is typical of many US citizens. My host families were not avid churchgoers, and yet I wish to characterize the New Zealanders that I met as religious. They love wearing sweaters and casual clothes, and many look uncomfortable in ties and suits. They are generous and considerate of others, and they love animals. Finally, they enjoy a good time, and they have a delightful sense of humor. To illustrate the humor I found, I share the following true story:

Shortly after our arrival in New Zealand, each team member was assigned to a Rotarian's home, and I learned that I would be staying with Jack Lions and his wife, Carol. Our GSE team training cautioned us about the use of humor in a different area of the world, so I was careful to avoid commenting on the obvious age difference between Jack and his wife. Jack, about seventy years of age, appeared to be at least twenty years older than Carol. In the course of the evening, they revealed that their recent marriage was the second for each, and Carol seemed to be quite content with a husband twenty-five years her senior. As bed time approached, Jack asked me what I would like for breakfast, and I replied: "Whatever you are having would be fine." He then insisted that I choose from a number of selections, and I chose fruit, cereal, and coffee. Next, he wanted me to decide on a precise time to eat, and I said: "Good grief, Jack, I'll eat whenever you eat!" He said he planned to eat at 5:00AM, and Carol would be eating at 7:00AM. I quickly replied that I would eat at 7:00AM, eating my breakfast with Carol. For me, the thought of a 5:00AM breakfast was not a consideration, especially after completing my long flight to New Zealand. For some unknown reason, Carol laughed at my response.

As we prepared for bed, Jack pointed out my bedroom, and he indicated where he and Carol would be sleeping. He then reviewed the breakfast schedule, saying that he would eat at five, Carol would eat at seven, and I would eat at eight. I corrected Jack by saying I would have breakfast with Carol at seven, eating fruit and cereal with my coffee. At this point, Carol was laughing hard enough to bring tears to her eyes. Confused by the situation, I asked Carol to please tell me the "rest of the story." What was going on here? She finally caught her breath and said: "Ever since Jack and I got married, he has made it a habit to serve me my breakfast in bed each morning."

The next day, our GSE Team attended the weekly meeting of Jack's Rotary Club, and Jack had the nerve to make the following statement to his club's members: "What do you think of a Rotarian from the United States coming into your home and insisting on having breakfast with your wife in bed?" Club members naturally groaned and turned thumbs down, and the Sergeant-at-Arms came to me to collect a $5 fine for my improper behavior. As I paid the fine for what Jack said, I stated in a loud voice: "All I have to say is that I really enjoyed my breakfast." Laughter resounded from all parts of the room. I now knew the level of humor in New Zealand.

Two other examples of New Zealand humor come to mind. One Rotarian told me that they bury lawyers at sea, because down deep, lawyers are not all that bad. Another New Zealander was anxious to tell me that in our older years a man needs three things, a car, a television, and a wife, and they should all be working. When I returned to my home in Westminster, Maryland, following the GSE trip, I told my wife the three things needed in my retirement years, and she immediately quit her job as Volunteer Coordinator for the local Carroll County Farm Museum. Sharing humor with a spouse can at times prove to be a dangerous thing. Pictured below, Carol and Jack Lions joined me in Orlando, FL, for Rotary's '92 Convention, and it was for us a joyous reunion.

THE PYRAMIDS LED ME TO ELIZABETH PETERS

In the summer of 1998, my daughter and I were considering a possible trip to Egypt. Jennette was a travel agent, and she could arrange a FAM trip with GATE 1, leaving on Sunday, October 11, 1998. We would depart New York City via Egypt Air, arriving in Cairo on Monday, October 12. I had no idea what a FAM trip was, but we were made an offer we could not refuse!

The trip as arranged by GATE 1 sounded ideal, and the price was right. The only cause for my hesitation was the possibility of terrorist activity in the Nile Valley. On November 17, 1997, Islamic fundamentalists killed 58 foreign tourists in a massacre at the Temple of Hatshepsut in Luxor. Tourists had attended a performance of Verdi's "Aida" in Luxor a month earlier without a terrorist act, and their safety was assured by the Egyptian President, Hosni Mubarak. The killings proved otherwise, and the terrorist action impacted on the tourist trade, doing great harm to the economy of Egypt. Jennette and I decided to join the tour, believing that terrorists should not dictate our options in life. Had we known at that time that an Egypt Air 767 jetliner, flying from New York City to Cairo, on a Sunday in October of 1999, would crash off of Nantucket Island, killing all 217 passengers, we might have made a different decision. In other words, a terrible terrorist act occurred one year prior to our visit to Egypt, and another would occur one year after out return flight.

Our flight to Egypt in October of 1998 was pleasant, and we were in a new aircraft. On our approach to the Cairo Airport, the television screens showed the passengers the land surface ahead of us. We had the same view as that of the pilots. A camera must have been mounted on the nose of the plane. I could see the Nile River and the green strips to each side of the Nile. Beyond the irrigated strips were the desert areas, stretching to the east and to the west. On the west side, I saw tiny triangles in the sandy area, quite close to the green strip. The triangles I saw proved to be pyramids, and I had my first glimpse of the famous Pyramids of Giza from the air. We checked into the Sonesta Cairo hotel for dinner and a good night's sleep. The next morning, we would fly from Cairo to Luxor.

On a map, one notices that Egypt is divided into three parts: Lower Egypt, Middle Egypt, and Upper Egypt. Those of us from the United States are so accustomed to upper being north that we sometimes expect Upper Egypt to be the portion nearest to the Mediterranean Sea, and that is not the case. The Nile River flows from south to north, and it is the longest river in the world, about 4,000 miles in length. The fertile soil on each side of the Nile is narrow, several miles in width or less, sometimes called the "black land." The desert area was known as "the red land." Cairo is located in Lower Egypt, where the Nile separates into two branches before emptying into the Mediterranean Sea. Giza is just west of Cairo, and 15 miles to the south is Memphis, the ancient capital of Menufer.

Our flight from Cairo took us south to Luxor. Our tour arranged for us to visit most of the wondrous sights from this point in Middle Egypt to the Aswan Dam area in Upper Egypt. We traveled by boat on the Nile to Aswan, and the views from the boat were not dissimilar to views seen thousands of years earlier by the early Egyptians. The small mud huts, oxen drinking water from the Nile, and the crude fishing vessels, all depicted life as it must have been 3,000 years earlier. Urban areas and bridges across the Nile were almost non-existent in this part of Egypt.

The ancient temples and tombs of Egypt cannot be adequately described in these pages of my memoir, but my fondest memories in Middle and Upper Egypt include visits to The Temple of Karnak and the Avenue of the Sphinxes; The Temple of Hatshepsut, the tombs of Tutankhamun, Ramses, and Seti 1, and the Colossi of Memnon on the West Bank (the Valley of the Kings & the Valley of the Queens); the Temple of Horus in Edfu; and the Aswan Dam.

The 1998 Karnak photograph seen below was one of those taken by my daughter, Jennette. Her picture of the Avenue of the Sphinxes is not shown, but that location has to be a top tourist attraction, along with the Valley of the Kings, where some 64 Egypt Pharaohs were buried. The "High Aswan Dam" was completed in 1971, but smaller dams had been in existence since early in the 20th Century. Life after the construction of a dam at Aswan was much more stable for the Egyptians, and the tragic floods of the past could now be avoided in the Middle and Lower Egypt areas.

The Temple of Karnak

In Lower Egypt, my favorite memories include visits to the Pyramids of Giza and the Sphinx, the Egyptian Museum, the Hanging Church, and the Mohamed Ali Mosque. The Cairo Museum is a must for any visitor to Egypt. The mummies are thousands of years old, and the collections of priceless objects from tombs and pyramids are beyond belief. Those items from King Tut's tomb are perhaps the main attraction for most visitors, unless they are on temporary loan to other museums. The mask of King Tut is the most recognizable of all of his belongings, those belongings that were to carry him into the next life.

The Pyramids of Giza and the Sphinx represent the only surviving member of "the seven wonders of the world" as identified by the Greeks. The Pyramid of Cheops (Khufu) is the largest of the Giza pyramids, which date back more than 4,000 years. Some 2.3 million blocks were required to build the pyramid, the blocks averaging 2.3 tons. This Great Pyramid was 460 feet high, but now it measures 450 feet in height, the decrease in size caused by the loss of the casing stones, which originally covered the entire pyramid. The second in size is the Pyramid of Khafre, and near its peak, the original casing stones are still in place and quite visible. The much smaller pyramid is the Pyramid of Menkaure. My youngest son, John, died in April of 1997, and daughter Jennette placed John's picture deep between the stones of the Great Pyramid on our visit in October of 1998. It was a very touching gesture on Jennette's part. The face of the Sphinx was apparently carved in the likeness of King Khafre, and the blowing sand has caused damage to the structure over the many centuries.

Our tour group is pictured below, and behind us can be seen the Great Pyramid of Giza and the Sphinx. Our rather large group contained many travel agents, and that caused us to be given the royal treatment in every way. Our safety was never in doubt, and to emphasize the point, armed guards were always visible.

A jeep led our bus through the streets, and four armed men sat in the open jeep. Another armed guard stood in the front part of the bus. As our bus pulled away from the Great Pyramid of Giza, we observed a scary event. A young boy was running along the blocks of the pyramid, about six levels above the ground. He should not have been there, and he should never have been running. To our horror, he fell down the face of the pyramid, bouncing on each level of blocks until he landed on the ground. Many of us thought that he could not survive the fall, but after a short while, he got up and ran away into the crowd. We all cheered and returned to the bus.

The food on our trip was especially good at the large hotels, but only fair at other locations. The beverages were a point of concern, and bottled water and bottled soda were a necessity. I was under the weather for part of the boat ride on the Nile, and I believe that the beverages caused my distress. A Belly Dance was scheduled on board the boat, but my distress caused me to miss the show. Jennette also felt ill for the last few days of the trip. On one occasion, I placed my used glass on a tray with soiled dishes, and the waiter on the boat started to fill the same glass with juice for another tourist. I took the glass away from him, and told him that the use of dirty glasses could cause others to be ill. My rebuke did not influenced him in the slightest.

When I returned home from the tour of Egypt, I wanted to read mystery novels and other literary works that related to the country that was now vivid in my mind. A librarian in Westminster, Maryland, asked if I had ever read the novels of Elizabeth Peters. I had not, and that day, I began reading one of the series of books in the Amelia Peabody collection. I have now read all of the eighteen books starting with the first in the series, keeping them in the proper order. In the award-winning novels, Amelia and her handsome husband, Radcliffe Emerson, do annual excavations in Egypt, covering a period of 35 years, and they frequently encounter murderers and illegal antique racketeers along the way. All of the novels written about the Emerson family's exploits in the Land of the Pharaohs have allowed me to retain the memories of my own 1998 visit to Egypt, and Elizabeth Peters quickly became one of my favorite authors.

I was a bit surprised to learn that the author's real name was Barbara Mertz, and that she wrote under the names of Elizabeth Peters and Barbara Michaels. I was further surprised to learn that her residence, when not traveling to Egypt, was located just a half-hour drive from my own home in Westminster, Maryland. My father once ran an auto repair shop in Liberty, the small town nearest her home, and my mother attended the college that awarded Barbara an honorary degree, Hood College in Frederick, Maryland. My efforts to meet Barbara over lunch or at one of her book signings have all failed, but Barbara has been kind enough to correspond with me on three or four occasions. I treasure her friendship and I am grateful that her novels remind me of my memorable tour of Egypt in 1998.

MARRIED LIFE EXPERIENCES

My wife and I are celebrating our 50th Wedding Anniversary this year, in the year 2010. We must be having fun, because it is said that time flies when you are having fun. The first of five memoirs relates how wife Carol and I met in 1959, and the last memoir describes the newest member of the Shook family, namely our 115 pound dog, Shadow. The Shook family of Westminster, MD, is pictured below (minus Shadow). Left to right, they are Carol, Jennette, Ken, Bill, and John.

John was the youngest family member, and his death in 1997 was very difficult for all of us to accept. At some point, I'll need to generate a memoir about the impact that his tragic death had on family members and other friends.

ARTIST JOHN LEWIS VISITS THE USA IN 1958

John Lewis at Loch Lomond

One of my great benefits from the two-year obligation to serve in the US military was an opportunity to use my leave time to visit many of the countries of Europe. And one of my benefits of the tour of Europe was the opportunity to become friends with an English artist, John Lewis. John was an art teacher in Birmingham, England, and we met at Loch Lomond in Scotland. John was on vacation from his classroom, and we quickly found we had much in common. Both were dedicated to education, and we loved to travel. I was more into dramatic art and music, but John's obvious talent in painting and sculpture was easy to appreciate. He would sketch his favorite scenes, while I snapped photographs of Loch Lomond and Ben Lomond. "Loch" as you know is the word for lake, and "ben" refers to a mountain peak. This destination was a side trip from Edinburgh. John invited me to join him in Birmingham for a steak dinner, and we planned the suitable date.

Following my visits to London and to Stratford-upon-Avon, I journeyed on to Birmingham to see John. He took me on long walking tours, and we spent several hours in his school. John asked many questions about our schools in the United States and about art programs in particular. I did not read between the lines, but he would later make his intentions quite clear. He wanted to seek my help in arranging a visit to the United States. John's walk was very distinctive, as he leaned slightly forward and his hands were firmly clasped behind his back. Today when I copy his walk, his image comes back to me. John prepared an excellent steak dinner for me that day, and I stayed the night before departing for Norwich, England and a flight to Paris.

After my tour of Europe, John Lewis was a faithful letter writer. We kept in touch, and I supported him in his quest to journey to the States. Finally, I wrote that he could stay at the college where I worked, and John could visit secondary schools in Maryland on my admissions schedule to recruit college applicants. The Birmingham School System saw how John would benefit from the experience, and John was given a leave of absence and a stipend toward expenses. John arrived at the Baltimore airport in 1959, and we had a joyous three weeks together. John used his free time to do watercolor paintings of the college campus, and two of those paintings were placed in my admissions office when he departed for England. John also gave me a metallic sculpture, which I prize today.

Perhaps John's greatest gift to me was that he enabled me to meet my future wife. The question of how married couples first meet is a popular inquiry in our society, and my story is a bit humorous and somewhat unique. John wanted to see a college art class in session, so during his stay on campus, we decided to see an evening art class. The class was a combination of undergraduate students and graduate students, and all were doing watercolor paintings of a fruit arrangement. We stood in the back of the hall, and rows of students were in a semicircular pattern around the fruit display. John and I were discussing that later that night we might view some of my European slides, taken on my European trip in 1957. The graduate student standing directly in front of us overheard our comments, and she turned and said that she had also been on a tour of Europe in April and May of 1957. I introduced her to John, and she invited us to her Westminster home to view the slides. She also had many colored slides from her tour, so the evening became a long one. Carol and her parents were very nice, and John and I enjoyed our time in the Jennette household. John would soon return to England, but my visits to the Jennette home would continue. Carol and I married in the campus chapel in June of 1960.

* * * *

A John Lewis painting in my Admissions Office

BUYING OUR FIRST HOME AT AUCTION

If you expect me to enlighten you on the art of bidding at auctions, skip this memoir and move on to the next episode of interest. Actually, I confess that I am very uncomfortable at sales with competitive bidding and fast talking auctioneers. One of my few purchases of this type took place at a recent "silent auction." Many items were on display at the Carroll County Community College Book Fair. A book-publishing firm, Random House, was the sponsor of the annual event, and many autographed books were available for bids. A "New York Times Bestselling Author," Elizabeth Peters, sent me a signed copy of her book *The Golden One*, and I added it to the table of items. In case you are not familiar with "silent auctions," visitors to the fair can record a bid on any object provided the new bid is higher than any earlier recorded bid. Late in the afternoon, I checked on the highest bid for the book by Elizabeth Peters, and I checked on the highest bid for another book written by golfer Ben Crenshaw. I put in a bid on each book. Several days later, I was informed that only the golfing book was mine, and it was a real bargain at $35 for a copy autographed by Ben Crenshaw.

People who conduct auctions are always happy to see my wife arrive at any auction they conduct. They know that Carol is the one person to point to when the bidding slows down. When an auctioneer gives her a pleading look, her right arm immediately stretches to the heavens, signaling a bid. I refuse to drive a truck to an auction, because my wife might try to fill it. I tremble when she returns from a sale, eagerly telling me of her good fortune at finding remarkable bargains. The only question in my mind is:

How can we spend all of the money that her bargains save us? Carol's purchases (of things that we can't do without) fill our garage, our basement, our attic, and every room and closet in the house. I demand (perhaps suggest is a better choice of words) that she remove two objects from the house for each new addition she brings into the house, but as you perhaps know, husbands seldom win such arguments.

Carol and I were married in June of 1960, and we found a beautiful second floor apartment at 37 ½ West Green Street, Westminster, Maryland. It was a perfect first home for us, and we even had a garage under the house for our one car. We had a first floor entry and a second floor entry, both requiring that we climb a flight of stairs. We were young in the early 1960s, and the climb was no bother to us. Within a year, however, our first child arrived, and many more objects had to be carried up those steps. In 1963, our thoughts of owning a home began to emerge. The apartment still served our needs, but we wanted our rent payments to go toward the purchase of a home. In addition, we longed for space for a back yard, allowing for a swing and sand box. A yard would make it possible to acquire a family pet, preferably a female Lab. Carol and I agreed that a family was not complete without a dog. While at 37 ½ West Green Street, we did acquire a sandbox for Bill, and Bill and I assembled the sandbox outside the apartment's entrance. Heaven only knows where it could be stored, since we had no yard space. The entrance to the garage was on the opposite side of the building, having a connection to an alleyway.

In July of 1963, a home located at 47 West Green Street came on to the market, and it was just a few doors away from our apartment. The house was an ideal size for our growing family, and the building was in excellent condition. It had a third floor attic, and the second floor had one large bedroom, two small bedrooms, and 1 ½ baths. On the first floor, there was a large living room, a large dining room, a large kitchen, a small study, and a sizable entry area. The house also had a full basement, a side porch, a one-car garage, and a nice backyard. I admit the house was rather plain in appearance, but it did have aluminum siding. The house was exactly as it appears in the attached photograph. I was disappointed to learn that it would be auctioned off to the highest bidder, and this nearly turned me away. I decided to at least make an appearance at the sale, and there was a typewriter that interested me.

The sale was on a pleasant day, and I walked the few steps from 37 ½ West Green to 47 West Green Street. Some 30-40 people were surveying the objects up for sale. Some of the smaller items were sold, and then the first bids were made on the house. I waited until there was a pause in the bidding, and I then entered a slightly higher bid. When no one else gave the auctioneer a nod, I assumed that the house was mine, but that was not the case. The auctioneer then said: "Bidding on the house will resume in one hour." This delay was very upsetting, but I waited the required hour. When bidding was resumed an hour later, no one spoke. The auctioneer, in frustration, then decided to add the window air conditioners, as part of the sale. Once again, no one attempted to top my bid. Finally, the auctioneer ended the action by shouting: "Sold!" He then had the nerve to ask for bids on the same air conditioners that he had added to the house sale. I asked him about this strange behavior, because my bid had acquired the house. He said: "You did not enter another bid, so the air conditioners never became part of your purchase." In other words, he wanted me to bid against myself.

The bad taste left in my mouth by the auctioneer's actions did not last long, because Carol and I had acquired a very nice home for the reasonable price of $23,200. As I later stated to everyone, I truly went to this auction to buy a typewriter, and I ended up buying the house. The price of the house was a real bargain, in my opinion, but keeping in mind that the year of purchase was 1963, the transaction was not what some might have called "a steal." If my memory serves me correctly, my college salary in 1963 was less than 1/3 of the selling price of the house that we had purchased at auction. The move from our apartment, just four doors away, to 47 West Green Street was a sight to behold. Many things could be carried the short distance by hand, and a station wagon was needed for the larger furniture. To enhance the house's appearance, my father built a white picket fence to enclose the back yard, and I added black aluminum shutters to all of the many windows in the front of the house. The final modification was to plant bagged Christmas trees on each side of the front walkway. Those pine trees would eventually grow to be taller than the house. The transformation was complete.

Our final two children, Jennette and John, were born while we lived in our first home, the 47 West Green Street property. It is often said that people do not forget the first boyfriend or girlfriend, the first kiss, and the first car. Perhaps buying your first home, especially if bought at a public auction, belongs on the list.

Moving into and enjoying our first house

WE WERE A ONE-CAR FAMILY IN THE 1960s

Early in my married life, my wife and I shared the use of a family car. In the first part of the 1960's, this was not an unusual condition for young married couples. If both partners in the marriage were employed outside of the home, sharing one car took much thought and careful family planning. The trend toward more women in the workplace was an established fact of the 1950's and the 1960's, but mothers with young children still favored a stay-at-home role.

My employment as a college admissions officer required frequent travel to secondary schools in a six state area, and some travel forced me to be away from home for three or four successive days. A college car was generally made available for my use. On these occasions, my wife could have full use of the family car, provided I had a way to get to the campus to pick up the college car. My admissions travel was especially heavy during the months of September, October, and November, and a dedicated effort on my part could yield a successful recruitment year. My young son often gave me a send-off as I departed from home. One morning, he reminded me of the possible negative impact of business travel on the family when he said "Daddy, thank you for coming." It was hard for me to focus on my school visits that day.

In a lighter and more humorous vein, I can still recall an occasion when I employed logic to solve a minor transportation problem. On that particular day, I was interviewing student applicants on campus in the morning, and the late afternoon schedule was unusually light. I decided to leave work early and walk the short distance to my home. The weather was pleasant for walking, and I saw no reason for my wife to drive to the campus to pick me up in the family car. Rather than phone my wife (the easy way out), I decided to use superior logic to determine the route I would walk from the college to my home. If I reasoned correctly, I would select the exact path my wife would drive, if she drove to the campus to pick me up. In that way, I could intercept her before she arrived at my office. I quickly sketched the map shown on the next page, and the logic began to flow. West Green and West Main ran east and west, and an alley ran parallel between these two streets. I did not diagram the alley, because my wife would not select an alley for her drive to the campus.

The one-way streets also reduced the options open to my wife (she seldom drove the wrong way on a one-way street). If you have looked at the sketch, you correctly concluded that there were three choices for my wife to consider. She had to use Green and Main streets, but she could select King's Lane or Maryland Avenue or New Windsor Road to connect the two streets. I decided that New Windsor Road would be the choice, and that was the route I walked from campus to my home.

I felt confident of my decision as I walked home that afternoon, and at no time did my wife drive pass me heading in the opposite direction toward the college campus. My wife was in fact at home when I completed my pleasant walk, but my car was not there. The car was back at the college. It seems that I had driven the family car to work that morning. Quietly, without Carol knowing, I slipped out the back door of the house and quickly covered the distance to the campus to retrieve the family car. My logic was not at fault that day, but the original premise was incorrect. My wife had not kept the car that day!

Hand-Sketched Map - College to Home

JUDGING BEAUTY CONTESTS, 1970s and 1980s

I suppose that everyone has witnessed beauty contests, and it is only natural that we try our hand at guessing which contestant will win the crown. We are sometimes shocked to find that our favorites fail to reach the final five, and we wonder if the judges are biased for some reason. On other occasions, our selections hit the mark, and we congratulate the judges for their wisdom. If you have never been a judge at such a pageant, I can tell you that it is quite an experience. I have been a judge at both local pageants and state pageants, and the selection process can be quite complicated. Beauty pageants are no longer based solely on physical beauty, as the reader is certainly aware. Contestants are often rated on things such as talent, personality, ability to communicate, and community service projects. Beauty and poise are still essential, if the winner is to fulfill a future public relations role for the pageant.

My role as a judge for beauty contests was partly a result of my employment background. I was a Dean of Admissions & Financial Aid for Western Maryland College for seventeen years, and following that, I served as Executive Director of the Maryland State Scholarship Board for ten years. In both roles, I needed to guide high school students in the college application and selection process, and financial aid was often a critical element in that decision-making. Another possible factor that motivated pageant directors to seek me as a judge was the fact that my wife had been a former "Miss Maryland," and she was in the "top ten" the year that Lee Meriwether won the "Miss America" title. My wife (below left) was Carol

Jennette at that time, a student at Wake Forest University. She and I were later married in 1960. After our marriage we were able to return to some of the reunions in Atlantic City held for contestants of prior Miss America Pageants.

Beverly Ann Smith
Miss Maryland
'1962-63'

At least three other "Miss Maryland" winners had been students at Western Maryland College. One was Beverly Smith (above right), and one was Kathy Neff of Cumberland, Maryland. She later worked as a member in my College Admissions staff, and Kathy's campus photo as shown below was used for the cover of one of our brochures.

Local pageants that I judged were enjoyable. Those of us serving as judges knew that many of the girls were appearing on stage before live audiences for the first time. Indeed, most of the contestants were understandably scared and often lacked self-confidence. Considering the circumstances, the more experienced judges would help to calm the contestants and provide each girl with a worthwhile learning experience. The interview session was a perfect spot to accomplish this, as each girl shared with judges her interests and future goals in life.

My childhood town was Frederick, Maryland, and Frederick had numerous spots of natural beauty and historical importance. At Frederick pageants, I liked to ask

contestants where they would most like to take friends who visited the Frederick area. The answers I wished for never came. It would have been nice to have contestants mention the home of Barbara Fritchie, the grave of Francis Scott Key, the home of Roger Brook Taney, Frederick's historic churches and museums, or perhaps Braddock Heights with its beautiful view of the picturesque Middletown valley. Nearly all contestants said that visitors would be taken to a local mall. Some local pageants had few girls competing, and sometimes the local winners had no chance at the state pageants.

State pageants often tend to gain a lot of news coverage, and in some states, the final night has television coverage. On a visit to Hawaii in late June, my wife and I happened to watch TV coverage of the Miss Hawaii Pageant finals. The winner that year did well in Atlantic City, and like most winners at the state level, she needed to elevate herself in order to reach the ultimate goal at the national level. Vanessa Williams seemed to be the perfect candidate in 1984, and she was an African-American. She won the "Miss America" crown only to later lose it for a violation of pageant rules. Phyllis George was "Miss America" in 1971, and her title helped her to be successful as a sportscaster, an entrepreneur, an actress, and Kentucky's First Lady.

My reflection on beauty pageants would not be complete if I failed to mention a particular episode of a 1960s TV show called "The Twilight Zone" with Rod Serling. That show made me realize that beauty is truly in the eye of the beholder, and this realization made me a better judge of beauty contests. The Rod Serling episode had surgeons struggling to change the facial features of a man and a woman, who were apparently badly deformed and might never be allowed to live with normal-looking members of that particular society. Try as they might, the surgeons finally had to give up the effort as a failure, and all persons in the operating room screamed in horror at the sight of the two faces being unwrapped. The man and woman operated upon would be forced to move away in hopes of locating a spot where their looks would not frighten others. In the closing scene, the faces of the male and female patients are revealed, and the two faces would easily meet any Hollywood standards for glamour. Why were they then viewed as objects of pity by the surgeons and other medical staff? The surgeons and medical staff removed their masks and all of their faces were hideous and grotesque in the eyes of the TV audience, but not in the eyes of residents of that society which had a different concept of beauty. Now, I put you to the test!

In selecting a group of persons for readers to judge and rate for glamour, I decided to focus mainly on the best known stars of Hollywood in the 1960s and 1970s. I admit that movies of this time frame did not provide a true sampling of the beautiful people of all races and cultures, but it was the period that I most frequently served as a judge for beauty pageants. Times have changed, I agree, but my personal opinion of beauty and glamour has changed little over the decades. If you are a senior citizen, you will no doubt remember enough of the names to rate the actresses and actors. If you do not remember persons on the lists or if you are a younger person then please check with older relatives or check the names on Google. com search. Have fun!

Concluding Remarks and Final Ratings: I begin by saying that I regret that I could not provide lovely photographs of all persons on the lists to assist you in the ranking process, but I feared that some of those photos might violate copyright laws. My wife had the urge to add some names to the lists, but I told her that was a "no-no." The men she would have added were: Michael Douglas, Henry Fonda, Harrison Ford, Rock Hudson, Jimmy Stewart, and Spencer Tracey. She would have added actress Joan Crawford. Regarding Rock Hudson and Joan Crawford, I would have agreed.

When you look at the rankings that follow, you will note that Carol and I agreed on three male stars and on

How would you rate these twelve actresses and twelve actors for glamour? (Rank 1-6, where 1 is best.)

Cyd Charisse	Catherine Deneuve	Greta Garbo
Ava Gardner	Shirley Jones	Grace Kelly
Nicole Kidman	Hedy Lamarr	Marilyn Monroe
Ginger Rodgers	Elizabeth Taylor	Loretta Young
#1_____	#2_____	#3_____
#4_____	#5_____	#6_____

Warren Beatty	Charles Boyer	Marlon Brando
Richard Burton	Sean Connery	Errol Flynn
Clark Gable	Cary Grant	Lawrence Olivier
Gregory Peck	Tyrone Power	Robert Redford
#1_____	#2_____	#3_____
#4_____	#5_____	#6_____

three female stars. Younger readers may not have the benefit of age, and true, concepts of beauty have changed over the years since the 1960s and 1970s.

My wife's actress rankings were: 1) Elizabeth Taylor, 2) Grace Kelly, 3) Cyd Charisse, 4) Ava Gardner, 5) Loretta Young, and 6) Greta Garbo. Her ranks for actors were: 1) Sean Connery, 2) Richard Burton, 3) Tyrone Power, 4) Cary Grant, 5) Warren Beatty, and 6) Robert Redford.

My actress selections were: 1) Hedy Lamarr, 2) Catherine Deneuve, 3) Grace Kelly, 4) Elizabeth Taylor, 5) Greta Garbo, and 6) Cyd Charisse. For actors: 1) A tie between Clark Gable & Errol Flynn, 3) Tyrone Power, 4) Lawrence Olivier, 5) Cary Grant, and 6) Robert Redford.

THE TRAGIC LOSS OF A SON

It is said that one of the ways to cope with a tragic event in life is to share it with others, and writing a memoir is a possible option. At one point, I had decided not to include a memoir about my son's death in this book, but to ignore it would be to ignore an important happening that had a major impact on our family. Life is not always fun and laughter, and into each life some rain must fall.

It was a pleasant day in April of 1997 when I drove John to the Shock Trauma Center in downtown Baltimore, and on this Thursday, John was saying goodbye to his doctors and nurses after years of treatment to rebuild his leg. Years earlier, he had been injured while riding a motorcycle. An elderly lady had turned into his lane of traffic, not seeing him, and her car drove him many feet into a neighboring yard. He was taken by helicopter to Baltimore's Shock Trauma Center, where a surgeon finally decided to save the leg rather than amputate, and recovery would extend for years. John still had pain and physical limitations in April of 1997, but on this final visit, he walked up and down the hospital hallway giving hope and encouragement to patients waiting for treatments. John drove me to the Baltimore airport that Saturday, and my flight was taking me to Ecuador to arrange a Rotary project in that country.

On my second day in Ecuador, my wife had somehow managed to locate me, and her phone message was that John had died in his sleep. The cause was cardiac arrhythmia. While in a state of shock, I discussed that a quick return flight would be almost impossible to arrange, and Carol said I could return as late as the following

Friday, one day before the funeral service. My brother, Charles, was the pastor for the Saturday service which was attended by an overflow audience. People of all ages came to pay their last respects, and some younger friends placed inside the casket drum sticks and favorite stones that belonged with John.

Carol showed great strength during this time and hid the pain felt by any mother facing such a family tragedy. Jennette and Bill, as sister and brother, also hid their pain, and they welcomed the many visitors to the service. My feeling of shock would remain for at least another week, and I found it extremely hard to focus on everyday matters. An old car that I purchased for John sat outside our garage for several years before I could part with it. John's room remained untouched for many months, and at times, I nearly looked into his room expecting to see if he and our dog were lying on his bed. They often slept together.

John died at age 27. One of Carol's prize photos was one taken of John at Beaver Lake in New Jersey, and it is shown below. This wonderful picture reveals John's love of nature, and it also contrasts his adult appearance with that of his younger years as shown in the family photo on page 73 of this book.

SHADOW'S TRIAL PERIOD

In 2007, the Airpark Animal Hospital listed the Species as Canine, the Breed as Mix, Labrador Retriever (Part Great Dane), the Weight as 101.30 pounds, and the Patient Name as Shadow. Actually, Shadow was not a patient at the Hospital, but Dr. Herrick brought the dog there for me to pick up, suggesting that Shadow would be a perfect household pet for the Shook family. Dr. Herrick knew that Carol and I loved dogs, and he knew that our last three family pets, Jessie, Holly, and Talley, had all been Labs. Jessie had died months earlier after a series of seizures, and Carol stated that she wanted no more dogs. For her, this was the typical reaction after the death of a family pet, but when I brought home each new Lab that was "free to a good home," she quickly learned to love the animal.

I had no idea of what to expect when I came for Shadow. In fact, I was surprised to hear Dr. Herrick's voice on the phone when I called the "free to a good home" number listed in the local newspaper. Herrick said he had the dog at his farm, and he was trying to find a good home for him. In preparation for Shadow's trial period with us, Herrick said he would take him to the Airpark Hospital for all required shots and a bath. When Shadow was delivered to me in the waiting room on the day of our first meeting, I could not believe my eyes.

Shadow was the most perfect physical specimen of a dog that I had ever seen. Our past Labs had been mostly blondes, and never had they weighed more than 40 or 50 pounds when wet. Shadow had the size of a small thoroughbred horse, carrying well over 100 pounds on his strong legs. He had a black shiny coat and beautiful white markings on his chest and on all four paws. A colorful kerchief was attached to his powerful neck, making him look like a Christmas package. My dog leash, which was for a dog in the 60 to 80 pound range, would not do the job. When he jumped up to lick my face, I fell back several feet, reminding me of my high school football days. Had Dr. Herrick been present, I may have reconsidered taking Shadow home with me that day. Shadow came with his own crate, one that he seemed to have outgrown, and I questioned if the need was for a stable rather than a crate. At home, Carol, too, was shocked by Shadow's image, and she thought his white markings made him appear to be wearing a tuxedo on his body and spats on all four feet.

I learned to adjust to the presence of this massive creature, and we were amazed that he never knocked over furniture, destroying all in his path. He had amazing body control, and he lived up to his name of Shadow, always wanting to be tight against you. True to the Lab tradition, Shadow was gentle in dealing with our 4 year old granddaughter, Reanna, and he allowed her to lay her body all over his. Shadow's first flaw became known to us when he torn three rainspouts off of the back of the house. He apparently grabbed the lower end of each spout and backed up, pealing each 30 to 40 foot section off of the building. Perhaps he saw a tiny chipmunk run into the spout as some suggested, but we had no choice but to replace the missing rainspouts with water barrels. Shadow's second flaw was that he was found to be allergic to certain foods, especially foods that had low price tags. Dr. Herrick suggested that we feed him a special blend of dog food that could only be purchased at the vet's office, and each 28 pound bag would cost about $82.

Dog owners run into a problem whenever they attempt to travel and use their time-share properties. The Days Inn motels sometime welcome guests to bring along their pets, but time-share properties almost never allow pets on the grounds. The only exception to such rules would be allowances made for seeing-eye dogs. On one occasion, Carol and I took Shadow along to Carol's Wake Forest University reunion, and things worked out pretty well at a nearby Days Inn. I expected that we would be assigned a first floor unit with easy access to an outdoor grassy area. To my surprise we were given a third floor room, and we needed to enter through the main lobby, taking the elevator to our room. Others staying in the Inn appeared a bit shocked when Shadow attempted to say hello to everyone in the lobby. Thank heavens he did not try to give each a lick. Shadow enjoyed the elevator rides, but he kept hitting the wrong floor button. Shadow was great in the car, and he filled the entire back seat. When he stood up, he naturally blocked any views through a rear-view mirror. Carol often said while driving "I wish Shadow would sit down on the back seat," and I usually responded to her "Carol, he is sitting down."

In planning a recent trip to use our time-shares in Williamsburg, VA, we decided to have a young college girl act as our dog sitter (and house sitter) while we were away. It was a good decision, and the cost was about what we would have had to pay for Shadow's kennel care at the Westminster Airpark Animal facility. Every few days, the dog sitter would call us in Williamsburg to report on Shadow's behavior, and she and the dog got along beautifully. I asked where Shadow slept at night, and she said several nights he slept in his crate and several nights he slept on the bed, his head resting on her back. During one phone call, I asked her to place the phone next to Shadow's ear, and I spoke to him about being a good dog. When she came back on the line, she said that he must have recognized my voice, because he began licking the phone.

In the original discussion with Dr. Herrick, the starting date of the "Shadow's trial period" in the Shook household was clear, but the ending date was left a bit vague. Nevertheless, I feel certain that "Shadow's trial period" has finally reached a conclusion, and all decisions have been made by the parties involved. Unlike trial periods in the past, this time the pet seemed to demand an equal voice in the decision making process. Shadow possibly evaluated us more than we evaluated him, and after weighing numerous factors, Shadow decided to make the Shook household his permanent home. Carol and I are both happy with his decision, and we will comply with his three conditions: 1) The red and black University of Maryland blanket originally slated to go to son, Bill, will now be viewed as Shadow's blanket; 2) Shadow will have daily access to my bed between the hours of 8:00AM and 10:00PM; and 3) Shadow will never be fed low-priced dog food, and his two daily meals will be served at precisely 7:00AM and 4:00PM, or earlier if possible. Carol and I placed our signatures at the bottom of the agreement document, and Shadow affixed his paw print.

[One photo below shows Shadow attacking a slightly-used backyard rainspout, and the other photo reveals that Shadow often shares my bed at nap time.]

OCCUPATION RELATED EXPERIENCES

In the year 2010, the down-turn in our US economy caused everyone to be concerned with unemployment figures which approach the 10% level. My first choice of a memoir for this category will be read by you as a sharp contrast with this employment reality. The second memoir experience exposed me to Bennett Cerf for several years, and my instruction to a group of Random House employees made this possible.

The other memoirs in this occupation category are grouped as either related to my experiences as Dean of Admissions of Western Maryland College or related to my role as an administrator of college student aid programs. In my admissions role, I must have processed nearly 18,000 student applications over my eighteen years of college employment, and from that large group, I now offer you four case studies of applicants that still remain vivid in my memory, after the passage of three decades. Later, I list several admissions "giants."

One memoir related to student financial aid matters is entitled "An Evening With Oprah In 1982," named to catch your attention. Its earlier title was: "The Night I Lost Out To Wall Street Week." The impact of Russia's Sputnik 1 on federally-funded college-student financial aid programs is covered in the other memoir.

NEVER APPLYING FOR A JOB

I find that I enjoy sharing stories about experiences that I have had in my day-to-day living, and it is my opinion, that most other people enjoy sharing their experiences as well. For this reason, I eagerly agreed to conduct workshops on the topic of *Memoirs*. My college studies mainly focused on subjects like mathematics and sociology, but writing and sharing memoirs has become a great interest of mine, and I have read the available literature on the topic. I even spoke to the person I recognize as the leading authority on memoir writing, William Zinsser of New York, and he and I have exchanged correspondence. At my workshops in Maryland, I often quote Mr. Zinsser's best advice to memoir writers by saying: "Think small."

These workshops were and are often held at public libraries, and sometimes I hold sessions at regional book fairs. At one such book fair, I asked a panel of local dignitaries to join me. None claimed any knowledge of memoirs, and for that reason, we met at my home days prior to the workshop to discuss the topic of memoirs. The panel members enjoyed refreshments on the side porch of my home, and within the hour, everyone was sharing personal stories that deserved to be preserved as memoirs. Those in the photo below are (left to right): Panelists Jean Worthley, Doris Pearce, Don Riley (& Mrs. Riley), and Ken

On the night of this particular session, which was held at the local Community College, Jean Worthley asked me to share with the audience my experience of "never applying for a job." I agreed to honor her request, but until that very moment, I had not thought of the topic as a unique experience worthy of memoir status. I shared the following experiences:

I attended Western Maryland College from 1948-1952, and I attended Wesleyan University from 1952-1954. Before entering each institution, I considered applying for employment, because limited finances made attendance at these colleges anything but a certainty. Scholarships awarded to me saved the day, and I was able to complete studies for both a Bachelor's Degree and a Master's Degree. At this point, in the spring of 1954, I received a phone call from the Superintendent of Schools in Madison, New Jersey, and Mr. McLean said that I was the person he needed to teach mathematics in Madison High School. I said that I did not know where Madison was, and I mentioned that my Maryland draft board was breathing down my neck. That draft board had allowed me time to attend graduate school, but they could call me to service at any moment. He said: "We'll pay your way to visit. Come and we'll just talk!" I went for the visit and loved Madison. I signed a contract to teach, and the 1954-1955 school year was not interrupted by a call from the draft board. In the summer of 1955, I asked the draft board to call me quickly so that my two-year military obligation would only impact on two school years and not three. My request, if approved by the Board, would allow me to return to Madison High in September of 1957.

The draft board would not cooperate by drafting me that summer, so I immediately enlisted to serve my two years of mandatory service. I did not view that action on my part as an application for employment. Nearing the conclusion of my two year stay at Fort Monmouth, which was located near Red Bank, New Jersey, I received a phone call from Dr. Lowell Ensor, President of Western Maryland College. That was my Alma Mater located in Westminster, MD. Dr. Ensor said that the College needed a person to form the first Admissions Office in the history of Western Maryland College, and I was seen as the "perfect candidate" for the position. He and the Dean of the Faculty, Dr. John Makosky, came to this conclusion after studying a short list of potential candidates. I said that I was flattered by the offer, but explained that I was obligated to return to Madison High in September of 1957 since the school had held my teaching position open for me until my military discharge. Dr. Ensor said: "Come and just talk." I went for the visit, and finally agreed to take the job provided it would not start until September of 1958. The College agreed to my request for a delay of one year, thus allowing me to return to

Madison High to teach in the Mathematics Department for the 1957-1958 school year.

My employment at Western Maryland College began in the summer of 1958. In addition to my admissions obligations, I volunteered to teach some mathematics and sociology courses, so I was a member of the faculty and a member of the administration. The wearing of multiple hats would be a personal characteristic I would never relinquish. At the end of my first year, I brought in a sizable entering class, and Dr. Ensor called me in to his office to award financial grants and loans. He had awarded all such grants in past years, and most such aid categories were summarized at the back of the WMC Catalogue. Since I was very familiar with the needs of the new entering students, all of my recommendations were adopted. As fast as he gave approval to an award of a grant or loan, his secretary, Helen Ohler, would record the action. She would later write letters to the students receiving aid. At the conclusion of the meeting, Dr. Ensor said that my admissions duties should be expanded to include all student financial aid awards as well. His role in the activity would cease at this point. I'm not sure that he fully realized that at that moment in time I occupied a one-room office on the second floor, and my one secretary was only available to me on a part-time basis. Some adjustments were made to ease the situation.

I believe the year was 1966, or thereabouts, when the President of Frederick Community College called me to ask that I consider being his assistant in Frederick. Since Frederick, MD, had been my home town, his call had a certain appeal, but the community colleges of the 1960s faced numerous problems. They lacked adequate financial support, and the entering students were generally viewed as those not *acceptable at colleges granting bachelor degrees. He said: "Just come and talk," but I declined his kind offer.*

In 1975, I received a phone call from the Chairman of the Maryland Scholarship Board, Mr. Robert Taubman, saying that I was the person best prepared to fill their Executive Director role. Mr. William Anthony was vacating the post and I was requested to "Just come and talk." My seventeen years as Dean of Admissions and Financial Aid at Western Maryland College had brought me great joy and love, and the decision to leave would be quite difficult. I visited with Mr. Taubman, and the challenge of the new role won me over. I started the new job in 1975, remaining there until 1985. There were many accomplishments in those ten years, but when Mr. Taubman retired from his Board Chairman position in 1985, my work at the Scholarship Board would also terminate.

In 1985, I received a phone call from top administrators in the offices of the federal grant and the federal loan programs located in Washington, DC. These programs were designed to assist needy students pay the mounting costs of higher education. These federal administrators were friends of mine, and they explained that their offices were facing a freeze on new hirings. Nevertheless, they wanted me to join them as a contract worker. What was needed was for a college or educational organization to honor the contract by acting as a go-between. Salary payments would go to the Westminster educational institution (Western Maryland College, Carroll County Community College, or the Carroll County Board of Education), and that institution would then pay me for my services. The college or school board would be paid funds to cover all expenses that it incurred to do the paper work.

The thought of commuting from my home in Westminster to an office in the District of Columbia was not appealing to me, but I would have followed through on such an arrangement had the local educational institutions cooperated. At first, everyone said they faced no problems with the arrangements, but later there was a dragging of feet for a variety of reasons. I finally decided to bring matters to a halt by accepting a teaching position in the local Carroll County School system. My remaining years prior to retirement in 1995 would therefore be devoted to teaching Algebra and Geometry and coaching the Girls High School Tennis Team. I did complete the necessary documents to teach in the Carroll County school system, so that action could be said to be the first time in my life that I ever applied for a job.

BENNETT CERF CAME TO WESTMINSTER, MD

In the 1960s, Mr. Bennett Cerf was a frequent visitor to my home community because Random House had a large distribution plant in Westminster, Maryland, and Bennett was visiting as the firm's principal owner. He and one other person founded the company in 1925, and the publishing firm apparently reached a value in the millions of dollars. Bennett got most of the credit for the firm's success, and he gained fame for his humor and wit. His puns, found in numerous collections, were enjoyed everywhere, and the correct reaction to these funny one-liners was to groan rather than laugh. I often shared his humor with my Westminster Rotary Club members, and the Rotarians would react not with laughter but rather by dropping silverware on the floor.

When I first met Bennett Cerf in 1964 or 1965, I felt that I already knew him, because of his regular appearances on the popular television program *What's My Line?* I first met him at a Random House reception, and he was interested in hearing about my training sessions for his plant employees. My classes focused on the application of sociological principles to leadership and motivation in the workplace. Our conversation then moved on to his love of humor, and he was delighted when I recited these puns from his published collections:

1. He knew he was going to get caught making graffiti. The handwriting was on the wall.
2. Time flies like an arrow. Fruit flies like a banana.
3. A bicycle can't stand on its own, because it is two-tired.

4. Those who jump off a Paris bridge are in Seine.
5. When a clock is hungry it goes back four seconds.
6. A chicken crossing the road is poultry in motion.
7. NASA recently sent a bunch of Holsteins into low earth orbit, calling it the herd shot 'round the world.

At the conclusion of that Random House reception, Bennett Cerf was naturally given the opportunity to address the guests and plant employees. To the surprise of no one, he ended his remarks with a funny story about "cats on a roof." He had problems with the final punch line of the story, and he looked in my direction, as if seeking my help. Everyone politely laughed with Bennett that afternoon and not at him. His inability to finish the joke shocked me, and days later, the same thing happened on the Western Maryland College campus. I was the Dean of Admissions on that campus, and Bennett was the guest speaker for some group. He attempted to tell the same "cats on the roof" story, and when in trouble, he once again looked in my direction for help with the punch line.

When we spoke moments later, I made light of his memory lapse, but I sensed that his failure to complete the story really concerned him. When he approached me, he said "There's H. Kenneth Shook." His use of my full name seemed to be his way of saying that his memory was in good working order. After moments of silence, I took this opportunity to ask him about a supposedly true story. The true story had to do with his $50 bet that author T. Theodore Geisel could not write a child's story using only 50 different words. Geisel responded to the challenge by writing his all-time best seller *Green Eggs and Ham*. Geisel claimed that Cerf never paid off the $50 bet. Laughter was Bennett's only response to my inquiry, but I doubt the $50 was paid.

The "cats on the roof" story had many variations, but the one told by Mr. Cerf went something like this:

One of two brothers owned cats, and they ruled his life. He would never attend parties or travel, because the cats could not be left alone at home. His brother was quite upset with his infatuation with cats, so it was a surprise when he offered to tend the cats while the cat owner took a free trip to Europe. After long debate, the cat owner finally agreed to allow his brother to tend the cats, and he departed for Europe. The first night, he called the brother tending the cats to ask about their condition. The brother in the US was mad that such a call would be made from Europe, and he told the traveler to forget the cats and enjoy the trip. Two nights later, a similar call arrived in the US, and the brother in Europe was told that the cats were dead. The news overwhelmed him, and he hung up the phone and collapsed on his bed. Hours later, he redialed the US and spoke to his brother in a strong but calm voice, saying: I know that I have been too emotional in my relationship with the cats, but you should never have broken the news of their death as you did. You could have said: "They are out on the roof," followed by "They got wet," followed by "'We had to call the vet," followed by "They passed away in their sleep." He then asked the brother in the US: "How is mother?" The reply, after a lengthy pause, was: "At the moment, she is out on the roof. "

I was shocked to learn of Mr. Cerf's death in 1971, and

I could still hear him addressing me as "Kenneth Shook" or "H. Kenneth Shook" rather than using only my first name. My thoughts at that time were of the pleasant man I knew only briefly, and I was thankful for the times that we did have together. He always had a smile on his face and a twinkle in his eyes. On several occasions, I mailed sets of colored slides to him containing photos that I had taken during his visits to the Westminster community. Each time, he acknowledged my gift, and I believe he must have laughed when he began each note using my full name. Meeting him enriched my life.

Pictured below are one of his letters addressing me as H. Kenneth Shook and his Hollywood "Star."

RANDOM HOUSE, INC.

457 MADISON AVENUE, NEW YORK 22, N.Y.

TELEPHONE PLAZA 1-2600

BENNETT CERF
CHAIRMAN OF THE BOARD

September 28, 1966

Bennett Cerf's star

Mr. H. Kenneth Shook
Western Maryland College
Westminster, Maryland

Dear Kenneth Shook:

Thank you very much for the colored slides. I'll be taking them up to the country with me this weekend, where we have a projector, and will be thinking of you all while we're running the pictures through.

With cordial best regards,

Bennett Cerf

COLLEGE ADMISSIONS EXPERIENCES

My entry into college admissions work paralleled the period when many colleges were just opening admissions offices on their campuses. In the late 1950s, registrars were happy to turn over the responsibilities to others, and I enjoyed starting my job with a clean slate. With only a part-time secretary to assist me, I had to visit schools to recruit students, and I needed to prepare new admissions procedures for adoption. Without the aid of computer services, a visual board (shown with Kathy Neff in the photo) was used to track applications. Out of thousands of applicants that I encountered, my memoirs that follow will acquaint you with four admissions decisions that I'll never forget.

PREDICTING A COLLEGE APPLICANT'S SUCCESS

I began work at WMC in the summer of 1958, too late to have an impact on the entering class of 1958. A faculty committee would assist me in selecting the entering class of 1959, and all recognized the need for a reliable test to measure an applicant's aptitude for doing college work.

By the early 1960s, most colleges had created offices to handle the admissions operation, and applications were no longer mailed to College Registrars. For many colleges the number of applicants actually exceeded the available college spaces for new entering students. This was a glorious time for colleges, since only a percentage of applicants could be offered admission to colleges. To assist in the screening of applicants, Western Maryland College and most other higher education institutions began to require the Scholastic Aptitude Test (the SAT) of the College Entrance Examination Board (the CEEB). Most college applicants began to feel an increase in pressure, and to insure acceptance to a college, these applicants began to make "multiple applications." Some high school seniors submitted applications to as many as ten or fifteen colleges.

In addition to aptitude tests, many high school students also began taking a variety of achievement tests. The student's class rank was now appearing on transcripts with greater frequency, but secondary schools with a high percentage of graduates going on to college sometimes felt that their students were harmed by a college's use of class rank. They argued that students ranking in the second quarter of their classes were on a par with students from weaker high school who ranked in the top tenth of their graduation classes. The better admissions officers did take this into account, and they continued to view courses and grades as the best predictors of future college success. Class rank, SAT, PSAT, ACT, National Merit, and other achievement test results were added to the mix.

Entering Student Characteristics

Very Good H.S. Grades Very Good SAT Scores	Very Good H.S. Grades Just Average SAT Scores
Just Average H.S. Grades Very Good SAT Scores	Just Average H.S. Grades Just Average SAT Scores

The attached chart divides a typical entering college class into four quadrants based on high school grades received by the students and their scores on SATs. The upper left quadrant of the chart includes students who are high achievers and also have high scores on aptitude tests, while students in the lower right quadrant are average (or lower) in both grades and aptitude scores. The upper right group contains students who achieve good school grades but test low on aptitude tests, and the lower left group test well but do not achieve high grades in their class work.

College Applicant Rating Chart

For us at WMC, it came as no surprise that the high school students with high test scores and high grades tended to receive the best grades in college classes, and that the student group with the low test scores and lower high school grades tended to get the lowest college grades. As experienced admissions officers would have expected, the second best group of applicants was the group found in the upper right quadrant, those students with lower scores on aptitude tests but high achievers none-the-less. These students were often described as "highly motivated" and "hard working." The lower left group ranked third in academic success at the college level. These findings justify a college applicant rating chart such as that shown on the next page. The chart provided a plus or a minus rating for each applicant, based on high school rank and SAT results. Some colleges used a mathematical formula to rate applicants, but at Western Maryland we preferred the chart, and we often shared it with school counselors.

The next two pages discuss the application of the chart to certain admissions candidates. If you find it too technical, please move on to the next memoir. The chart lists the graduating high school ranks on the left. The top category is the highest 5% of a school's graduating class and the bottom category is for those out of the highest 40% of a class. The SAT results listed along the lower side of the chart are the totals of the verbal and mathematical scores (V + M). The score of 1400+ includes all totals in the range from 1400 to the maximum score of 1600. The lowest category would include totals below 900. As stated above, students in the lower right portion of the chart would most likely receive low grades in college, and students located in the upper left portion tended to receive the highest college grades. The stair-step design allowed us to extend the positive ratings into a portion of the upper right quadrant of applicants and into a portion of the lower left quadrant of applicants as well.

Visiting applicants and their parents were often shown the chart at my office, and sometimes they were

Selecting Students

Applicants (A, B, C, D, E, & F) can be rated by a chart using class rank ® and SAT scores. The more positive the rating the greater the expected academic success. Other factors for consideration: a) Subjects & grades b) Personality traits, goals, & motivation c) Recommendations by teachers & counselors d) Participation in non-academic activities e) Strength of the sending secondary school (% going to college and their success in college) f) Applicant's choice of a major area of study g) Student's impact of the cultural and geographic diversity of the entering class.

R/SAT	1400+	1350+	1300+	1250+	1200+	1150+	1100+	1050+	1000+	950+	900+	Below
1st 5%	+9	+8	+7	+6	+5	+4	+3	+2	+1	-1	-2	-3
2nd 5%	+9	+8	A +7	+6	+5	+4	+3	+2	+1	-1	-2	D -3
3rd 5%	+8	+7	+6	+5	+4	+3	+2	+1	-1	-2	-3	-4
4th 5%	+7	+6	+5	+4	+3	+2	B +1	-1	-2	-3	-4	-5
5th 5%	+6	+5	+4	+3	+2	+1	-1	-2	-3	-4	-5	-6
6th 5%	+5	+4	+3	+2	+1	-1	E -2	-3	-4	-5	C -6	-7
7th 5%	+4	+3	+2	+1	-1	-2	-3	-4	-5	-6	-7	-8
8th 5%	+3	+2	+1	-1	F -2	-3	-4	-5	-6	-7	-8	-9
Below	-1	-2	-3	-4	-5	-6	-7	-8	-9	-10	-11	-12

asked to act as if they were members of the admissions committee, thus voting on candidates A, B, C, D, E, and F. The applicant designated A on the chart was rather quickly offered admission, unless some non-academic factor or student personal trait was found to be overwhelmingly negative. Likewise, applicant C was a quick rejection. B looked like a "Yes," and D looked like a "No." E and F, on the other hand, were candidates usually viewed as borderline applicants, and these cases were thought to require campus interviews and possibly additional senior year grades before a final decision could be reached. It was pointed out to the visitors that the strength of the secondary school could also move a borderline applicant up or down. A school that annually sent 80% of its graduates on the college was generally viewed as stronger than a high school that sent only 25% on to college. Borderline applicants desiring to major in a field of study that few other applicants were seeking would have a greater likelihood of acceptance. The reverse was also true, when applicants sought majors that were already crowded with qualified applicants. In interviewing students, I often pointed out their position on the chart, helping them to better visualize the academic challenge they faced at WMC. In some cases, the student wisely decided not to apply for admission. Some students with negative ratings on the chart still wanted to apply, and I of course allowed it. They were advised to apply to at least a few other colleges to insure at least one college acceptance offer.

The student evaluation chart which we used at WMC in the early 1960s and 1970s was both effective and accurate.

TWO TALENTED FEMALE APPLICANTS

A typical Admissions Committee of Western Maryland College is shown below, and this particular group included our Faculty Dean, the Dean of Students, three Department Chairs (Physics, Music, and Biology), and three Admissions Office staff members. Borderline applicants were the Committee's greatest concern, especially if children of alumni.

In the year 1972, two highly talented female applicants caught my attention, and they caused me a bit of concern. I honestly wondered if Western Maryland College was to be their best choice as a college to attend in 1973. Our applicants since the early 1960s were very impressive, and this was especially true of female applicants. The male applicant group was always quite respectable, but their group did tend to lag a bit behind the female group in numbers and quality. Why then was I so concerned about these two female applicants? The two were clearly outstanding students, ranking very high on the chart that we used to evaluate applicants. Beyond that, they even wanted academic majors that were not crowded with WMC students, programs that we wanted to expand. Most admissions officers of that time period spent their time worrying about applicants that appeared to be too weak to survive the academic demands of their colleges, but the same concern needed to be expressed for those rare applicants who were found to be at too advanced a level of training, a level of training that was well beyond the preparation of students typically found in that college's entering class. I was asking myself the question: Should applicants ever be refused admission because they are too bright or too advanced in their academic pursuits?

If a student goes off of the positive ratings scale of a typical entering class chart, should that applicant be discouraged from attending that particular college? In fairness to the two girls being discussed, I first wanted them to meet with their Department Heads, the faculty members who would have the greatest impact on their academic studies at the college. Before making a college choice, they needed to inquire about the possibility of additional courses to meet their unique needs and the possibility of individual one-on-one instruction in their major fields. One of the girls was interested in music, and the Chairman of the Music Department was thrilled to meet his talented applicant. He could hardly contain his enthusiasm, and he began to project programs and projects that were not listed in the College Catalogue. Following that successful meeting, I then urged this young woman to complete enrollment procedures, and she did. I had no doubts that she would get a fine education at WMC, and that following college, she would also achieve great success in her music career.

Carol Fulton, the girl just discussed, is pictured below. She became a successful music major whose talents blossomed during her college years. Carol could have

chosen from many elite colleges, but her choice was Western Maryland, and the decision was one that she has never regretted. Carol married a Western Maryland classmate, and she has had a highly successful career.

In the case of the second female applicant, the woman occupying the Art Department Chair did not react with enthusiasm when I introduced her to her talented applicant. The Chair was polite but blunt with her remarks, asking: "What am I supposed to do with her?" She made it clear that this student was too advanced to fit into the existing program, and there were no prospects that special classes would be considered in future years to accommodate such a talented student. The applicant, in the Chair's opinion, should attend a college elsewhere. Based on the Art Department Chair's comments, I naturally urged the girl not to enroll at Western Maryland College, but she did not follow my advice. She attended WMC for the next two years, but then transferred to a nationally recognized art college for her final two years of under-graduate training.

ANOTHER NORWEGIAN HAS ENROLLED

In the spring of 1972, a student at Western Maryland College walked into my Admissions Office on campus and asked if a friend could still apply for admission. As the College's Dean of Admissions & Student Financial Aid, I was proud to announce that Western Maryland had closed its enrollment for the fall semester of academic year 1972-1973. I could also have added that we had the enviable record of closing enrollments before nearly all other colleges in the Middle-Atlantic region. High school seniors in the six surrounding states knew this to be true, and this impressed potential applicants, knowing that Western Maryland College was the "first choice college" for many other college-bound students. The College's "rolling admissions" procedures gave applicants a prompt acceptance or rejection decision by the Admissions Committee, and as a result, it was not uncommon to find that those enrolled in our Freshmen Class had often applied to Western Maryland College and to no other school.

The WMC student standing before me was Odd Haugen, and his body filled the doorway. He was a handsome Norwegian lad, standing about 6' 3" and weighing perhaps 230 pounds. Odd said that his friend was in Norway, and Odd had recommended Western Maryland College to him. The friend was Knut Hjeltnes, and Knut had recently decided that Brigham Young University would not be a wise choice for him. Since foreign students add much to a college campus, I agreed to contact Knut, and we phoned him in Norway to discuss the matter. From an academic viewpoint, he seemed to meet our admissions standards, but he would need financial assistance. I decided to allow Knut to apply for admission.

After receiving Knut's application materials and other official documents, I prepared his offer of admission. Before sending it, I spoke to Dr. Lowell Ensor, President of the College. I proposed to Dr. Ensor that we offer Knut a "Foreign Student" scholarship, and he quickly supported my suggestion. The President understood that all regular aid had been awarded weeks earlier, but he saw the value in creating this new category of student aid and gave his approval.

Knut and Odd were delighted to learn that Western Maryland was willing to add an additional student to the College's 1972 entering class, and the "Foreign Student" aid grant would make it possible for Knut to enroll. Knut said he would attend Western Maryland, but later complications would force him to delay entry until mid-year. On the day of Knut's arrival at the Baltimore-Washington International Airport, Odd and I were able to welcome him as he walked off of the plane. Until that moment, I had no idea of Knut's appearance. Let me just say that seeing him for the first time, I was reminded of the well-known statue of David located in Florence, Italy.

Knut was a perfect physical specimen. Here was another handsome Norwegian, a blond this time, standing about 6' 2" and weighing some 210 pounds. Riding back to the College's Westminster campus took about 45 minutes, and Odd used the time to boast of his successes and the records he established in football and track. I had to laugh as Knut responded that he could improve on all of Odd's past achievements (running faster, throwing the discus further, etc.). If Knut's statements were true, I suddenly realized that we now had a Division I quality athlete on our Division III College campus. The boys from Norway had a great reunion and the entire trip back to Westminster was a joyous one.

The WMC Track Team of 1973 had an undefeated season, thanks to the presence of Odd Haugen and his friend from Norway, Knut Hjeltnes. Knut in that spring semester at WMC established Mason-Dixon Conference marks in discus, shot, and javelin. In a close duel with Johns Hopkins University, his Western Maryland coach asked him to enter the triple-jump event. This was a new event for him, but he won easily and helped to secure the victory. In late April of 1973, I remember reading a newspaper headline that referred to Knut as "Ironman Knut," and Knut would prove himself worthy of that title at the famous Penn Relays.

Rick Carpenter was Knut's track coach that year, and he entered him in the discus event of the 1973 Penn Relays. People processing the entry forms believed that the form had been filled out improperly, giving wrong information. Coach Carpenter had predicted that his Division III freshman would toss the discus about 188 feet. Penn Relay officials pointed out to the Western Maryland coach that such a toss would break the existing record. Rick replied that the entry form was not incorrect, and at the 1973 Penn Relays, Knut proved him right. Knut actually bettered the prediction by some five feet, tossing the discus 193 feet, creating a new record that would stand for decades. This Division III college athlete stunned all of the Division I college coaches and players, and Penn State University officials began pressuring Knut to transfer to their institution. Knut now qualified as the best discus thrower in the world, and he was in fact a member of the Norwegian Olympic Team.

Knut Hjeltnes

Odd Haugen, pictured below, also set records. His records did not quite match those of his friend, Knut, but he did hold the Middle Atlantic Conference record for the shot put, with a toss of 55′ 1″. After graduating from Western Maryland, Odd played some professional football and he later managed health spas in San Francisco and Hawaii.

It was a day in the spring of 1973, when Track Coach Rick Carpenter and I were watching the two boys from Norway as they enjoyed a campus dining hall meal. Rick said to me: "We will never again see the likes of these two athletes in our lifetime. We and Western Maryland College have been truly blessed."

Odd Haugen

Knut and Odd have shared their feelings on the matter, and both felt that they too were blessed by spending time on the Western Maryland campus.

A "SUMMER SCHOOL-FEBRUARY" ENTRY

In the early months of 2009, I made weekly visits to my foot doctor's office located in the Billingslea Medical Building in Westminster, Maryland. For a period of some ten weeks, I must have been one of the doctor's best customers. A total of six toe nails had to be removed, not all from the same foot, and Dr. Butler decided to check on my progress on a weekly basis. His enjoyment of my jokes and my memoirs became evident, and people in the waiting room could often hear his laughter during our closed-door sessions. Each visit was pleasant, but I made it clear that I was not willing to give up any more of my remaining four toe nails.

On one visit to the foot doctor, I was happy to see an old friend in Dr. Butler's waiting room. The friend was Gary LeGates, a former student at Western Maryland College. Gary was seated there with his seeing-eye dog. Gary was the first blind student that I had admitted to the College while I was serving as Dean of Admissions between the years of 1958 and 1975. Gary's blind girl friend also entered WMC at the same time. Gary and I chatted for a while in Dr. Butler's waiting room, and Gary reminded me that I had offered him admission to the College through a unique "Summer School- February Program," and he had gladly accepted that variation to the more traditional "September Entry."

I recalled that Gary entered Western Maryland College in the late 1960s, seeking entry at a time when WMC and most other colleges had an abundance of applicants to fill a limited amount of classroom and dormitory space on campus. Since Western Maryland filled available space in entering classes more rapidly than nearly all other colleges, I had introduced a "Summer School-February" approach as a means of admitting some 20 to 25 additional students from the applicant pool. My plan would enroll these students in our summer school, followed by a return to the College the following February. Some space was always available at those two points in the school calendar. By carrying 12 hours of academic credit in that one summer, the students would still be able to graduate with their class, the group that started in the more traditional way by beginning in the fall semester which generally started in September. Since WMC's summer school had a lower cost than that of the fall semester, the SS-Feb. students acquired the first year of schooling at a savings of hundreds of dollars, and that was a positive feature of the program. The College decided to implement my proposed "SS-Feb. Program," and a total of 50 or more students entered WMC through this unique program. Without the program, those students would have been forced to attend other colleges. Any applicant seeking another college as his or her first choice could have improved the odds of acceptance if entry at a time other than September had been mentioned as an option.

Gary and Ninette LeGates stroll the campus

Gary LeGates and his girlfriend, Ninette Mellott, were married after their graduation from Western Maryland, and for many years, Gary was a highly successful teacher in Westminster High School. While an under-graduate, Gary used only a white cane to fly about the campus, and his blind girlfriend was often by his side. On one occasion, I was close behind them and heard Gary remark: "I see you wrote a long letter to your family!" His choice of words caught me by surprise, but then I realized that Gary was carrying her mail in his free hand, and his fingers measured the thickness of the envelope.

Gary laughed at my story about his use of the white cane while a college student and his remark about Ninette's long letter to her parents. As he patted the head of his seeing-eye dog, Gary entertained those of us in the doctor's office by discussing his use of lights in his Westminster apartment. He installed a system which allowed him to know if lights are on or off, but he quickly added that the system was not always perfect. He admitted that there were times when he forgot to turn on lights after dark. Sometimes guests, seated in total darkness, needed to ask if lights could be turned on. Also, there were times when visitors came to their front door after dark, and seeing no lights, they incorrectly assumed that Gary and Ninette were not at home.

The presence Gary and Ninette on the campus contributed much to the Western Maryland experience.

THESE TWO MALE APPLICANTS LED THE WAY

A prior memoir in this cluster of memoirs stated that two special female applicants caught my eye in 1973. The same can be said about two male applicants who came to my attention in the fall of 1965. They caused my interest to peak because they were both sound applicants from Baltimore area schools, and they were both black students. In September of 1964, the first black student in the history of Western Maryland College enrolled and he was elected by the freshman class as their president. It was my hope that the two new applicants for 1965 entry, Joe Smothers and Victor McTeer, would enroll and lead the way toward a trend which would attract more minority students to this Westminster campus.

Western Maryland was founded in 1867, and its original charter said it was to benefit students: "without regard to race, religion, color, sex, national or ethnic origin." Females made up a significant portion of the very first classes, and Western Maryland College is said to be the first co-ed college south of the Mason-Dixon line. Over many decades, other races were welcome to apply and to enroll, but no black students actually enrolled in WMC until 1964. In the 1960s, our admissions procedures offered all applicants the same level playing field, but some colleges were being pressured to tilt the playing field in favor of minority groups. It was my hope that the first minority students entering Western Maryland College would not be borderline academic students, and for this reason, I was happy in 1965 that Victor McTeer and Joe Smothers were clearly acceptable on academic grounds. They were also fine athletes, and I assumed that playing on college teams would made their adjustment to campus life easier and more enjoyable. Their 1969 college yearbook photos appear below.

Joe Smothers   **Victor McTeer**

As I write this memoir in year 2010, I have had no recent conversation with Victor, but I had a delightful talk with Joe and his wife, Mary. Joe confirmed that financial aid was critical if he was to attend Western Maryland with its private school costs. My personal call to then Maryland Senator Verda Welcome was what made Joe's enrollment possible. The addition of her Senatorial award not only allowed Joe to attend Western Maryland, but Joe's family was then able to use its limited resources to finance his sister's education at Morgan State University.

Victor was larger in size than Joe, and he was the football player. His defensive skills won him Little All-American honors in football. Joe was a bit smaller than Victor, but on the basketball court, he could hold his own against taller players. Joe was honored at graduation by being selected a member of Western Maryland's select group called Who's Who.

In my conversation with Joe, I said that I had no knowledge of any unpleasant racial instances that involved Joe or Victor over their four years at Western Maryland, but Joe said that was not the case. I then expected such events to be rare and off-campus, but Joe said that some such encounters were indeed on-campus experiences. He was careful in his wording when he said: "Some students, and some faculty members, were simply not ready to accept a mixing of the races at Western Maryland, and this was especially true when mixed-dating between the races took place."

I continue to be proud of the positive impact that Joe Smothers and Victor McTeer had on the Western Maryland campus, and I applaud their success in later life. Joe gained recognition as a popular college professor in Baltimore for many years, and Victor received national prominence as a lawyer in Mississippi, promoting worthy causes for minority populations. Joe and Victor never relinquished their role of leadership, leading the way so that others could follow their example in seeking a better and more productive life. Well done! Well done!

COLLEGE ADMISSION REJECTION LETTERS

For a number of years, I enjoyed teaching a college course in Sociology called Demography. Perhaps because of my mathematics background, working with numbers and population pyramids was right down my alley, and knowing population trends was most helpful in my admissions work. Everyone knew about the population boom shortly after World War II, and any admissions officer worth his or her salt should have realized that the large population headed for college in the late 1960s was going to diminish in size in the early 1970s. The "Baby Boomers" would hit college campuses in the late 1960s, and more women would be seeking higher education now that being housewives was no longer their only option in life. Colleges needed to make a critical decision after 1965, deciding whether to expand to accommodate the many applicants or to hold enrollments steady and enroll brighter students. Colleges choosing to increase their enrollments had to consider the possibility that spaces might be hard to fill in the early 1970s when the applicant pool was predicted to shrink in size.

At Western Maryland College, where I was Dean of Admissions & Financial Aid, we chose to expand from about 1100 undergraduates to approximately 1400 students. This growth took place in the late 1960s. In the early 1970s, we were still able to bring in classes large enough to hold at the 1400 level. Some other colleges, however, miscalculated the extent of their drawing power, and their drop in applications in the early years of the 1970s forced them to close their doors. Students and faculty members at those institutions were as a rule shocked to learn of the closings, because college trustees often made such decisions in secret sessions. Students, faculty and alumni were often kept in the dark, and their points of view were never a consideration. Members of the graduating class in some cases completed their studies before the doors were closed. Under-graduate students and faculty members, on the other hand, had to begin a frantic search for another institution of higher learning that would meet their future needs. These abrupt closings caused some faculty members to be unemployed the next school year. Some students either terminated their college education or possibly enrolled in schools that could not meet their career goals. Anger and increased tensions resulted in chaotic situations in the early 1970s when some colleges decided to close their doors.

The "college rejection letters" shown on the next page are my version of two rejection letters that first came to my attention when they were printed in the _College Board Review._

<u>SAMPLE REJECTION LETTERS</u>
When the college applicant pool is large:
Dear Applicant: 4/13/68

Your application for admission to Prestige College has been carefully considered, and I regret that I must turn you down. You should understand that many fine students are seeking to enroll, and only a small portion of applicants can be accepted.

I feel that you do possess numerous redeeming qualities, and I know that there is a school out there that will fulfill your needs. Good luck to you in your future endeavors.

Very sincerely,
Dean of Admissions

When the college applicant pool is small:
Dear Dean of Admissions: 4/13/73

Your letter of acceptance to Prestige College has been carefully considered, and I regret that I must turn you down. You should understand that many fine colleges are seeking my enrollment, and only one can be chosen.

I feel that your college does possess numerous redeeming qualities, and I know that there are applicants out there that will fulfill your needs. Good luck to Prestige College in its future endeavors.

Very sincerely,
Worthy Applicant

During all of my seventeen years in college admissions work, *The College Board Review* was perhaps my favorite admissions journal, and on a number of occasions, they printed research articles that I had generated. The editors of that College Entrance Examination Board publication gave me great delight when they printed the two contrasting letters of rejection. In the late 1960s, the colleges were turning away many applicants, but in the early 1970s, the tide had turned. The shoe was now on the other foot, and strong applicants were rejecting numerous offers of admission, even admission to some of the more prestigious colleges. I extended my enjoyment of the rejection letters by quoting them when I spoke at many admissions institutes and workshops. The high school students and their parents that I encountered in each audience appreciated the message conveyed by the rejection letters, and they always responded to my remarks with hearty laughter, almost applause.

MY CALL TO WAKE FOREST'S BILL STARLING

In the spring of 1995, I was quite close to retirement, and my final year of employment included teaching high school mathematics and coaching the girls' tennis team. Happily, my final Westminster High tennis team won the 1995 County Championship, and the local paper said that I earned "Coach of the Year" honors. The paper also said that my ten years of coaching included 4 or 5 such tennis team champion-ships, but that may have been too high a number.

Our #1 singles player and our #1 doubles team did win county honors that year, and one of my senior players asked me to recommend her for entry into college. She was the type of person that most colleges would welcome with open arms. In this particular case, the girl was seeking admission to Wake Forest University, a Division I athletic university, and she realized that her athletic ability did not extend beyond playing at a Division III or possibly a Division II college. Since the Wake Forest Dean of Admissions was a close friend of mine, I decided to call him rather than write a letter of recommendation.

For some prestigious universities, the Dean of Admissions would have been quite difficult to reach by phone, but Bill Starling of Wake Forest made himself very accessible to the public. He took my call within a matter of minutes, and we reminisced a bit about our friendship of more than 30 years. Bill and I first met on the campus of DePaul University in 1959. We were both attending the first Admissions Institute ever held in this country, and as roommates, we developed a great friendship. I mentioned that I was engaged to a Wake Forest graduate,

Carol Jennette, and he was pleased to point out that he had dated her at Wake years before I met her. In the photo that follows, Bill and I are standing in the second row, surrounded by an all-star cast of admissions officers attending the 1959 Institute.

I told Bill that I had called to highly recommend one of his 1995 female applicants. Some of us in college admissions work had heard jokes about the clutter of materials in Bill's Wake Forest Admissions Office, but on this occasion, he had my tennis player's application folder in his hands within minutes. He said that she had an initial rating of an 83 on a 100 point scale, and naturally, I wanted to know what that implied about her possible acceptance to Wake. Bill's response led me to conclude that Wake sent acceptance letters to about 90% of those applicants rated 90 or higher, 70% of those in the 80s, perhaps 25% of those rated in the 70s, and possibly 5% of those rated below 70. I judged that initial ratings were mainly based on a combination of high school grades (or class rank) and SAT scores, and later changes to ratings were usually based on additional information gained from personal interviews and on meaningful recommendations. Applications were filed by category ratings, and members of Wake's admissions office staff continuously reworked the applications to place weaker applicants into the rejection file.

I would have enjoyed asking Bill about those candidates accepted with ratings in the low 70s and ratings in the 60s, but we remained focused on the applicant that I was recommending. Bill stated that my tennis player, rated 83, was a borderline case (not an automatic acceptance), and he asked about her tennis skills. I said that she was not a Division I tennis player, but that she possessed the qualities, academic and social, that would gain her success at Wake Forest. Her grades were high, placing her in the top 15% of a strong Westminster High academic class, and her test scores were well above average. She was a delightful person, and her quiet manner did not detract from her charm and positive impact on others. Her experience as a team player was a definite asset, and she and her family would fit nicely into the Wake Forest community. She and her family could afford the costs of the private University. Bill told me that he was placing a note into her folder, stating that no one should remove her from the active file without first consulting him. I shared Bill's encouraging words with the Westminster girl, and within a matter of weeks, she received an acceptance letter from Wake Forest and enrolled for the fall semester.

In contrast to the case discussed above, a decade later in the year 2005, I made phone calls to Division I universities in support of another Carroll County athlete, and this particular athlete in my judgment was capable of success in a lower Division I athletic program. One Division I university did show an interest in the girl but the University of Delaware had already awarded all of its scholarships. Another Division I university that should have shown an interest did not generate a meaningful response. If Division II colleges had been pursued, many would have made athletic scholarship offers to this fine player, but the girl decided instead to attend a Division III college. This female athlete was highly successful in her four years of playing ball for her Division III college team. She set numerous records and won awards, but I still wonder how she would have responded to the challenge of playing against teams at the Division I or Division II levels. My memoir readers should hear me say that academic programs of a college are more important than athletic programs when applicants choose a school to attend, but the increasing costs of higher education deserve to be in the mix.

* * *

Note: In the memoir that follows, Bill Starling's name is included in my list of giants among college admissions officers. Sadly, Bill died of a massive heart attack in 2001 after conducting an admissions workshop on the Wake Forest campus. Bill was completing his 45th year of admissions work for the University. His tragic loss was felt by the entire Wake Forest family and by those of us who knew him and shared with him the proud title of "college gatekeeper."

SOME ADMISSIONS OFFICERS ARE GIANTS

I like to refer to myself and others in the field of college admissions as "college gatekeepers," and out of the hundreds of college gatekeepers I have known some qualify as "Giants." The first two names that come to my mind are Jack Blackburn of the University of Virginia and Bill Starling of Wake Forest University. Not far behind would be the names of Mary Ross Flowers of Goucher College and Lucille Norman of Hood College.

Jack Blackburn, Dean of Admissions at the Un of VA

Jack Blackburn and his wife, Betty, pictured left, both

attended Western Maryland College at a time when I served as head of WMC's Admissions Office. Jack and Betty possessed all of the qualities to succeed in college and the potential for successful careers in college admissions work. I recall that both assisted us in the WMC Admissions Office during their undergraduate years. Betty once drew a picture to accompany the first admissions article that I ever wrote, and her sketch showed a student with luggage standing at a road intersection, hoping to catch a ride to a college campus. Jack mainly served us as a WMC campus tour guide in his undergraduate years. I was a bit surprised when I first learned that Jack was hired to head admissions at Mary Baldwin College, but I knew that he would love the work, and he certainly did. Jack next moved to the University of Virginia in 1979, and his selection by the University to be in charge of admissions in 1985 was a very high honor which he richly deserved. The University's faith in Jack was fully justified over the next 24 years, until his death in January of 2009. Many honors were bestowed upon Jack, and one was the Apperson Award. The Apperson Award is the highest honor our Chapter can bestow on a college gatekeeper. His calm and easy style won high praise from the many students he assisted in gaining admission to the University of Virginia. Jack will perhaps be best remembered for his efforts to recruit and to enroll minority and low-income students at the University. Jack ranks very high on my short list of "admissions giants."

Bill Starling, Dean of Admissions, Wake Forest

Bill and I first met at a 1959 College Admissions Institute. It was the first of its kind to be held in the United States, and we were both quite new to admissions work. Bill (pictured on the left) was scheduled to begin work at Wake Forest University and *I would be working at* Western Maryland College. Bill died of a massive heart attack in 2001 after conducting an admissions workshop on the Wake Forest campus. To honor Bill's 45 years of service to the University, the administration building now has Bill's name inscribed on it.

Bill would most certainly have received an Apperson Award had he been a member of our P & C Chapter of NACAC, but he belonged to a different chapter. No one could exceed Bill Starling for friendliness and helpfulness. He would stop in the middle of busy projects and busy schedules to take a phone call or answer an urgent request. People did joke about his cluttered office and the numerous piles of applications scattered about, but Bill had a system, and he could locate a document or application within minutes. A story, which I believe is true, relates that Bill's office window was broken during a campus celebration, and security guards reported to Bill that someone had gotten into his admissions office and had turned it upside-down. Bill hurried to his office, but he was happy to report that none of his papers had been disturbed. The office was as he left it. Bill's wife was present when I shared this humorous story on the Wake Forest campus, and she said that Bill knew nothing had been disturbed that night because a half-eaten sandwich he had left in his office had not been touched.

Student financial aid experiences

My duties as Dean of Admissions and Student Financial Aid ended in 1975. At that point, I departed Western Maryland College to assume new duties at the Maryland State Scholarship Board. As the Executive Director, I would be able to assist many thousands of Maryland residents to meet the costs of higher education, and legislators would turn to me for advice on proposed student-aid legislation. My ten year employment at the Scholarship Board would bring my years in financial work to a grand total of 27 years.

Although stories about the many applicants receiving grants and loans would provide heart-warming memoir material, confidentiality does not permit those stories to be told. That being the case, I offer you two memoirs in this category, namely "The Impact Of Russia's Sputnik 1" and "An Evening With Oprah In 1982."

THE IMPACT OF RUSSIA'S SPUTNIK

On October 4, 1957, the Russian Sputnik 1 was sent into orbit around the earth, and a month later, the Russians sent a dog into space. Do you remember what you were doing at the time? If you were living at the time, and possibly you were not, the event might not have held your interest, but the same cannot be said for people serving in Congress or those living in the White House. People running our government in Washington were set into a state of panic by Sputnik 1. In their eyes, the world now knew that Russia was ahead of the United States in the race to control space.

My reaction to the Russian success was not a state of panic, but had I realized the Washington group reaction, perhaps I could have foreseen new legislation to impact on high school and college instruction (especially the teaching of Mathematics and Science programs) and laws to change the future of financial aid programs for college students. In the 1960s, Congress justified its invasion of education systems as a "National Defense" mandate, and when defense was no longer an issue, the justification was shifted to "Educational Opportunity" for minority groups.

The early federally funded programs designed to aid college students took the form of loans, grants that need not be repaid, and work-study monies. At first, the college administrators had freedom to measure need levels and to make the awards as they saw fit. Later, as should have been expected, colleges had to conform to federal guide lines or get out of the tax-funded aid programs.

When I took charge of the Maryland State Scholarship

Board in 1975, about half of the states had no scholarship programs, but federally funded State Student Incentive Grants would soon force all states to enter the game. States could hardly say no when student aid funds were offered, and a match with state money was all that was required of the states.

In 1985, as National President of the State Scholarship Grant Programs, I was asked to offer advice and testimony on certain pending federal legislation, and federal control of student aid was often the topic to be addressed. The final shoe dropped in 1992, when "Federal Methodology" came into being. At this point, all other forms that had been used to determine a student's level of need would be pushed aside or used sparingly, if at all. Congress would never take its foot out of the door once the opportunity presented itself, so the federal dollars would direct the future course of college student financial aid programs, though at first, anyway, it seems to have been a "need."

AN EVENING WITH OPRAH IN 1982

My original title for this memoir was "I Lost Out To Wall Street Week In 1981," but I later decided that the new title shown above would attract the attention of more readers. Was I correct? After reading the memoir, you can decide for yourself if the change I made was justifiable.

I accepted the position of Executive Director of the Maryland State Scholarship Board in 1975, and one of the major goals of the Board was to convey financial aid information to all Maryland residents who were concerned about financing the costs of higher education. While at the Scholarship Board, I quickly discovered that Maryland newspapers, especially the Baltimore Sun, wanted to focus on controversy and negatives, and it was my hope that television, especially public television, would convey a more positive view of the total financial aid operation for college students.

In the late 1970s, I was invited by Jerry Turner to appear on his *Newsmakers* television program, and I was delighted to share that evening with Sister Kathleen Feeley, President of the College of Notre Dame of Maryland. Her school was said to be vulnerable because it was small, Catholic, liberal arts, located in the middle of a large city, and a women's college. Except for the middle-city location, I told Kathleen I liked all of her College's characteristics, and I hoped that her school would never change to a co-ed campus. Jerry Turner was the perfect host that evening, and he allowed me ample time to discuss current and future trends in financial aid programs for college students. I also had time to defend the majority of Maryland Senators and Delegates who awarded their State scholarships in a fair manner, not deserving the negative views that appeared in the press on a daily basis. I mentioned that some of my financial aid training sessions took place annually in the State House in Annapolis, and these popular sessions were always well attended by the Senators, Delegates, and their aides.

The financial aid community had many printed publications to address the procedures and pitfalls of college student financial aid, and many of us in the field visited schools and college fairs to make oral presentations. Beyond that, I felt that public television could provide a great service to the State by having a television program which focused on college student financial assistance. I knew of no other such TV program in the United States, but I urged Channel 67 to take the lead and undertake the project. I stated that the desirable month to run such a program would be January, a time which was several months prior to the deadline dates usually established by colleges and states for students to apply for financial assistance. This lead-time was vital, in my opinion, if students were expected to meet deadlines and if aid programs were to run smoothly and fairly.

Our Maryland public television station did not have an enthusiastic reaction to my suggestion for a program of student financial aid, but more discussions were held related to the content of such a presentation. I suggested the topics that needed to be included in the hour program, namely: the aid application form, the types of aid available, how aid packages were formed, and the costs of public and private colleges, and I suggested that institutional aid officers from various colleges should be present to take phone calls during the telecast. In addition, a small panel of aid experts could discuss different aspects of student aid programs and application procedures. Film clips could show how high school and college students successfully cope with the rather complex financial aid process.

After three years of interchange with Channel 67 in Maryland, I was told that a trial program on student financial aid would be run in 1981. I again mentioned that January would be the ideal time to air such an effort, because most aid applications are completed in the months of February or March. The Station selected a moderator for the program, choosing a TV or radio personality from the Baltimore area, and I acquired the panel of experts and the institutional aid officers who would answer phone calls. The first telecast went quite well, and later I received an excited phone call from Channel 67. The caller said that we outdrew all other TV programs that evening except for *Wall Street Week*, which just happened to be another program offered on Channel 67. My response was that I did not mind losing out to Louis Rukeyser's *Wall Street Week*.

No one at the time would have made a 1981 prediction that our financial aid program, named *You Can Afford College,* would actually outlast the long run of *Wall Street Week* on Channel 67. It continues to run in the year 2010. The program proves its value in helping students and their families as they struggled to meet the costs of higher education, but it may have also given a boost to one of the program's early moderators. In 1982, the moderator selected for our second annual financial aid program on Channel 67 was a Baltimore area news reporter named Oprah Winfrey.

Sharing the podium with Oprah that night in 1982 was a pleasant experience for me, and I often jokingly add, there can be no doubt that her exposure on that program contributed greatly to her future success. To support my claim, I point out that Oprah relocated to Chicago the very next year, 1983, hosting the "AM Chicago" television program, and the rest is history.

YOU CAN AFFORD COLLEGE '82

MONDAY, JANUARY 11
AT 9:00 P.M. ON

22·28·31·36·62·67
ANNAPOLIS   SALISBURY   HAGERSTOWN   OAKLAND   FREDERICK   BALTIMORE

STATIONS OF THE MARYLAND CENTER FOR PUBLIC BROADCASTING

In Maryland the cost for one year of college can be anywhere from $3000 to $10,000, making a four-year college education either unaffordable or a heavy financial burden for most students. But financial aid is available, even with recent cutbacks in federal funds.

"You Can Afford College '82" attempts to show high school students, their parents and all those desiring financial assistance for college how to obtain the available money. Produced at the Maryland Center for Public Broadcasting, this second annual, one-hour live special is hosted by Oprah Winfrey.

Students who have received funds for their education, as well as one who has not, are interviewed. A panel of financial aid experts, including Dr. Kenneth Shook, executive director of the Maryland State Scholastic Board, outlines the various types of assistance: state scholarships and grants, work-study programs, federal and private scholarships and loans.

During the program, viewers can phone in their questions about financial aid to the panelists.

maryland
center
for public
broadcasting

January 6, 1982

Dr. Kenneth Shook
Executive Director
Maryland State Scholarship Board

Dear Dr. Shook:

We would like to confirm your appearance as a guest on our up-coming
program "You Can Afford College '82." The show will be broadcast
live from 9 p.m. to 10 p.m. on Monday, January 11 at our studios in
Owings Mills. Generally, the format will include questions from the
program's hostess, Oprah Winfrey, directed to you and the other guests;
phone-in questions from viewers; and five currently completed film
segments focusing on four students now receiving financial aid and one
who did not receive aid. The topics will include: how to get financial
aid; what processes to follow; common mistakes by students, and recent
changes in the PELL Grant Program.

Please plan to arrive at the Center by 7:45 p.m. so we have adequate
time to do light make-up and discuss the elements of the program.

Since we have all color studio cameras, we ask that you avoid wearing
clothing that is white, beige, shiny or has highly contrasting colors.
Directions for reaching the Center are enclosed.

We look forward to seeing you on January 11.

Sincerely,

John Colston
Assistant to the Producer
PUBLIC AFFAIRS
337-4162

My thanks go to the Maryland Center for Public Broadcasting for providing these "You Can Afford College" 1981 and 1982 TV program photos and other materials. I also received a video of the 1982 program. Panelists included high school and college personnel and Oprah Winfrey was the program's hostess in 1982.

IMPACT OF SPORTS ON PLAYERS, COACHES, AND FANS

Sports have always played an important role in my life, and this was especially true after reaching high school age. At Frederick High, I played three sports as most good athletes were expected to do. I lettered in football, basketball, and baseball, but a bad knee injury in 1947 limited my future play to baseball seasons. Decades later, it is much more common to see players specialize in one sport, taking private lessons, and playing that one sport the entire year. Through my life, the transition was made from active player, to coaching, and finally, to being a parent of players and a fan of high school teams, especially women's volleyball teams.

Watching sports on TV has lost some of its interest for me, but the older professional golfers still hold my attention. I keep hoping the older champions will win just one more event before retirement has its way. For example, Freddy Couples and Tom Watson are the type of role models that I hope young athletes will pattern themselves after. Cal Ripken of baseball fame would also be a good choice for a role model.

I think you'll enjoy my memoir choices, and be sure to read about the baseball glove with two thumbs!

CONNIE MACK'S TEAM TRAINED IN FREDERICK

More than 60 years has passed since the spring of 1944, but I seem to recall the events of that spring as if it were yesterday. At that time, I was in the freshman class of Frederick High School, the only high school in Frederick, and when not thinking about the impact of World War II, I had optimistic thoughts of making the high school baseball team. My ability to hit a baseball was never questioned by my various coaches, but some questioned my choice of a fielding position. Some believed that only a left-handed thrower should play first base, and as you have guessed, I was a right-handed thrower who desired to play that position.

Since team members in those days provided their own gloves and spikes, I forced the issue by buying a three-pronged glove designed for the first base position, and I used that glove for the next two decades. It was the custom in those days to toss gloves onto the outfield grass and not carry them into the dugout between innings. My prized possession received no such harsh treatment, and my special bat was also given special care. Unlike the thin handled bat used by my idol Ted Williams, my choice was a thick-handled bat that carried the name of Rogers Hornsby. He and Ted both had season batting averages over .400, so my baseball expectations were high.

The banner headlines of the Frederick newspaper announced that the Philadelphia Athletics would be training in our home town for the months of March and April of 1944, and McCurdy Field would be the training site. This same field was used by the talented Frederick Hustler Baseball Team, and my Frederick High School baseball and football teams would also be playing future games at McCurdy Field. The Philadelphia players would reside in the famous Francis Scott Key Hotel, which was located some seven or eight blocks from the ball fields.

McCurdy Field's main diamond had a short left field fence, a distance of about 330 feet, if my memory is correct, and even I could hit drives that far at the age of fourteen. A fifteen or twenty foot screen was therefore placed atop that fence to add to its height. In sharp contrast, the distances to center field and to right field measured at well over 400 feet, so on occasion, a snow fence would be used to shorten those distances. The shortcomings found at McCurdy Field, plus Frederick's unstable weather conditions in March, were not ideal features for a spring training camp, but it was a choice necessitated by World War II and it was a choice that delighted most of our Frederick residents.

When the pro players checked into the Francis Scott Key Hotel in the spring of 1944, it was my good fortune to have a front row seat. The reason was that I held a job in Abe Ellen's Haberdashery, a clothing store that occupied the front corner of the Hotel. In addition to packing and unpacking boxes of clothing, I operated a steam press, pressing suits and pants for hotel guests. My older brother had held the job for several years, and you could say that I inherited the position from him. Ball players came into the shop, and some had their clothes pressed. It was fun to deliver pressed garments to the ball players' rooms in the hotel. On bad weather days, I sometimes could sit with players in the hotel lounges and listen to their stories. The experienced players dominated the conversations, and the rookies seldom found an opening to speak.

Some better known players, like George Kell and Bobo Newsom, were seldom seen in the lounges, and I believe that pitcher Bobo Newsom actually missed most of the 1944 spring training.

On one special occasion, Connie Mack was seated in the main lounge of the Francis Scott Key Hotel with his players, and he actually took the time to shake my hand. I recall how amazed I was with the strength of his grip. His firm handshake did not seem to match his rather fragile appearance. For me, that occasion became more memorable when the group began to discuss plans that were being made for a major celebration to be held later that year. The gala event would honor Mr. Mack for his glorious 50-year baseball career. The attached photo, courtesy of Bob Warrington and the Athletics Historical Society, shows a warmly dressed Mr. Mack seated by the McCurdy Field left field fence in 1944. The glove in his hand does not resemble gloves in use a decade later.

I must confess at this point that my favorite major league team in the late 1930s and early 1940s was the Detroit Tigers, and one of my prized possessions was the 1936 Baseball Yearbook which listed the Tigers as the 1935 Champions. That yearbook has been missing for many years, but I can still visualize the photos of Mickey Cochrane, Hank Greenberg, Charlie Gehringer, and Pete Fox, and all of them batted well over .300 in 1935. Their pitchers, as I recall, were Tommy Bridges, Schoolboy Rowe, and Elden Auker.

Reflecting on the Athletics' training camp in 1944, the one player who most stands out in my memory that spring was a rookie named Nellie Fox. He was sixteen years of age

and I was just two years younger. I was several inches taller and thirty or forty pounds heavier than this rookie. He and I were both right-handers, and both of us were seeking to make our respective teams at the first base position. Perhaps it was for these reasons that I identified with

Nellie Fox and rooted hard for this youngster's success. Due to his small size, he did look a bit out of place at first base, but I was happy to see him get his chance to play in a practice game against the Baltimore Orioles on March 26, 1944. I cheered when Nellie got a clean hit. Only later did I learn that that hit could be called "historic" in Fox's career. Some have identified it as his "first major league hit," and perhaps it was, but I will always remember Nellie's hit as his gift to me on my birthday. I turned fourteen on that date, March 26, 1944.

Frederick's McCurdy Field did not offer the Athletics the multiple playing diamonds they needed in 1944, and bad weather was another limitation on their spring training program. When the Athletics were able to hold practice sessions, many youngsters could be seen waiting outside the fences to retrieve foul balls. A foul ball could be used as the price of admission to the park or it could be retained as a souvenir. A broken bat was another prize item that was eagerly sought by spectators at the spring training camp.

The war years of the 1940s took their toll on professional sports, especially baseball, and many of the best athletes had to serve in the military. Charlie Keller, who made his home in the Frederick community, had his successful Yankee career interrupted by two years in the military, and Boston's Ted Williams missed nearly five years of baseball, while serving as a pilot. Frederick residents were able to see these great players play when their teams visited Griffith Stadium to face the Washington Senators. On one such occasion, I saw Washington outfielders catch two Ted Williams drives as each ball was about to clear the center-field fence, but a third William's drive was well beyond their reach.

When visits to a major league park were not possible, my grandfather and I would often listen to Arch McDonald broadcast the Washington Senator games. They were mostly afternoon games, and when my grandfather disappeared from the corn field, I knew I would find him with his ear pressed against the old Philco radio. Pop-Pop became very upset when radio static made listening next to impossible. Night games dated from 1935, I believe, but few night games, if any, were played during the War years. To our delight, Arch McDonald did air Senator away games, using Western Union wire to provide game details. You would have thought he was at the game, but actually, he used a drug store just three blocks from the White House to receive and forward game details. In these popular baseball broadcasts, he hit a gong four times for a home run and three times for a triple. What fun!

The impact of the war years on the Athletics was evident when watching the 1944 Spring Training Camp. Sixteen and seventeen-year-old youths were trying out for the team and some players in their late 30s and early 40s were trying to delay their retirement dates. Some major league teams signed players with physical handicaps, such as a one-armed player, and one team added a midget to the roster. The door was opened for women to play on professional baseball teams and in professional leagues. The Frederick baseball team known as the Hustlers actually benefited from the war-time situation when a player named Joe Moss joined the team. He was stationed at Camp Ritchie, MD, for his time in military service, and the camp was a short drive from Frederick. Joe Moss was not his real name, but I never learned his reason for the deception.

The baseball potential of Joe Moss was easy for all to see, and he later signed his real name, Ralph LaPointe, on a contract with the Philadelphia Phillies when discharged from the service in 1946. In one game, while playing for the Baltimore Orioles, he made six infield errors (a record I'm told), but he hit a homer in the ninth inning to win that game. Called up by the Phillies in August of 1947, LaPointe hit .308 for the rest of that season, making the 1947 Rookie All Star Team . Yogi Berra and Jackie Robinson also made that 1947 rookie team. The Phillies then traded LaPointe to St. Louis, acquiring Dick Sisler. For LaPointe, who was now positioned behind the Card's All Star Marty Marion, the 1948 season would prove to be his last in the Majors.

The Athletics Training Camp of 1944 is still vivid in my memory, especially the four or five inning NY Yankee game of April 5. A ticket cost $1.25, and it displayed a photo of Connie Mack and a rain date of April 6. No snow date was listed. On April 5, 1944, snow would halt the game, and some news papers reported that players then began throwing snowballs rather than baseballs. Sports writers loved the event for obvious reasons.

In that same year, 1944, I purchased my three-pronged first-baseman's mitt and my baseball career began in earnest. After eight years of high school ball and college ball, and another four years of playing summer league baseball, I served my two-year military obligation, stationed at Fort Monmouth, NJ. In 1956, I played for the Ft. Monmouth ball team, and as if by fate, my coach was Mule Haas. Six of Mule's twelve major league years were spent with the Athletics. His best year, 1929, was a World

Series year for the A's, and his average was .313, with 16 home runs and 82 RBIs.

At Ft. Monmouth, Mule took a special liking to me, and he often had me act as Team Captain. He shared his baseball past with me, perhaps because I was a bit older than other teammates. One newspaper photo showed Mule demonstrating to me his famous batting grip, and in a separate newspaper account, I was credited with a game winning triple. On that occasion, I won the game by hitting a triple with the bases loaded, and the ball was hit hard. It tore the glove off of the first baseman's hand, and the glove landed ten yards away, down the first base line. Upon my return to the dugout, Mule yelled loud enough for all to hear: "Shook, that's the way I used to hit the baseball!" Great fun!

The photo shown below was taken while I played for the Mule Haas Fort Monmouth Team of 1956. The picture is symbolic of the way I would want my baseball career to be remembered, with me playing first base, wearing my three-pronged glove. That glove, purchased in 1944 when the Athletics trained in Frederick, is still in the trunk of my car, and sadly, I see no way that it will end up in Cooperstown, NY, unless I drive it there.

Nellie Fox did make the Hall of Fame, but his first-base mitt did not make the journey with him, his second-base glove did. My thanks go out to Nellie Fox, Connie Mack, and other baseball coaches and players for my memorable experiences.

WINNING A GOLD PUTTER IN 1993

In 1993, the game of golf, along with tennis, had gained a position of importance in my life. Unlike earlier years of my life, I no longer played team sports, and individual sports were now the thing. I was coaching the Westminster High School's Women's Tennis Team in 1993, and I would have eagerly coached the Golf Team if the position had been vacant. My views on golf in the early 1990s are rather well summarized in the two paragraphs that follow.

Watching the professionals play golf is a joy to behold, but a greater joy is realized in actually playing the sport. Golf, unlike many other sports, is played for a lifetime. Most golf courses are appealing to the eye, and one can enjoy the scenery, even when the level of play is sub-par (less than desirable). It would appear that the typical golfer is the All-American type of individual, and the man or woman who plays the game is of high moral character and pleasant in personality. Most golfers enjoy winning, that is quite true, but they are gracious losers as well, generally speaking. Having said these things, I am proud to say that I am a golfer.

If you ask a golfer his handicap (strokes beyond par) and he begins telling you about his wife, then you know that he is not a competitive golfer. You should be able to beat his score, so concentrate on the other two players in your group. My handicap in 1993 could be as low as 7-9 on my home course, but add 6 strokes for harder courses. Some players claim to be able to shoot a score equal to their age, but most of us realize that this will never happen for us. As a slightly better-than-average golfer, I do not win a lot of tournaments, but the occasional good shot brings me back, week after week. I have won ten or twelve prizes and trophies for golf play, and most have been for "closest to the pin" on a par 3 hole. I have never had a "hole in one," but my wife was able to accomplish such a feat, and she will be happy to tell you that story. Once I hit a perfect drive toward a par 4 hole only to have the ball collide with a bird in flight. This almost never happens in golf, because birds seem to have a radar system for avoiding such collisions. The robin I hit gave his life that day, and I got a prize for *the most unusual birdie.* The Gold Putter was presented to me in 1993, and I received it because I hit "the worst shot of the entire tournament." All of the other golfers were eager to point their fingers at me until they saw the expensive Gold Putter. Only then did they remember other poor shots worth consideration.

The Gold Putter Trophy awarded to me in 1993 was made by a professional golfer, and he stated that the gold putter had a value of about $250. Owning such a valuable and unique trophy went a long way in helping me to over-come my embarrassment for hitting "the worst shot of the tournament." My crude sketch of the prize putter is shown on the next page, and its unusual features are fun to observe. The second sketch illustrates three types of shots made by a right handed golfer. For beginning golfers, hooks and slices generally indicate poor shots, but this would not be the case for most of the best players on the professional tour.

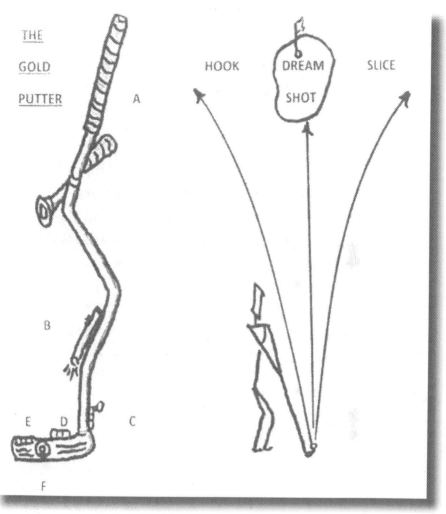

Gold Putter Diagrams

<u>Gold Putter Features</u>: A – Horn (to alert other players to be silent), B – Light (for night play), C – Tape Measure (to calculate ball-to-cup distance), D – Magnetic Compass (to sight the ball-to-cup direction), E – Balance (to keep the putter face level), and F – Sweet Spot (contact point for striking the ball)

For those of you waiting to hear more about "the worst shot" that won me the trophy, let me explain that the club slipped in my hand as I started the club in its downward path toward the ball. Had the nine iron not slipped in my hand, the ball might possibly have landed on the green, some 125 yards away. Instead, the slippage caused the clubface to turn clockwise, thus causing a shot referred to as a slice. My twisted club struck the ball in such a way that the ball was directed 90 degrees away from the desired flight path, and it landed innocently in the nearby highway, last seen bouncing in the direction of Baltimore City. I hasten to add that the ball's flight was not the cause of any known traffic accident, at least no accident was reported on that day. One additional word in my defense; I feel it is fair to say that even the best professional players would have had great difficulty stopping the club once it began it downward flight, and that includes Tiger Woods.

In the photo above, my powerful swing makes the club appear to be invisible, but the club's shadow is visible on the ground. Look hard!

THE BASEBALL GLOVE THAT HAD TWO THUMBS

[CONVERSATIONS WITH KELLY & GREG HARRIS]

Perhaps it was in the late 1990s when the name of Greg Harris first came to my attention, and if what I heard was true, he had accomplished something never done by any other baseball player in the modern era of the Major Leagues. For this and other reasons, I thought how wonderful it would be to meet him and perhaps say "Hello." He was an ambidextrous pitcher who actually made the big leagues, and apparently, he pitched with both arms in the same inning of a Major League game. I began to gather bits and pieces of information about Greg Harris only to learn that two big league pitchers had the same name and played during some of the same years. The one that I wanted was Greg Allen Harris, born November 2, 1955, and he played in the Majors from 1981 to 1995.

A bit of searching, combined with a bit of luck, produced a phone number and an address which could possibly have been those belonging to "my Greg Harris." If I was correct, I could call him in California and say "This is Ken Shook calling from Maryland," but for weeks, I could not build up the nerve to make the call. I did have unlimited long-distance phone service, so cost was not an issue. What concerned me was the fact that there seemed to be little justification for Greg to share any part of his valuable time with me on the phone. One night at about 11:30 P.M., I got the nerve I needed. I jumped out of bed and quickly dialed the California number before losing my nerve. The number actually rang a few times and then gave out a high pitched tone. To me, this meant the line was out of service. (Others later reminded me it could have been the phone's signal for receiving a FAX.) The next day, I decided to mail a package to the address in my notes, explaining my interest in Greg's accomplishments and stating my interest in writing memoirs. The next week, to my utter delight and surprise, a call came to my home from Kelly Harris, Greg's wife.

Kelly Harris related that Greg was on the road with the college team he coached, but that he wanted to talk with me when he returned home on Friday. She said I could call at 11:00 Maryland time. I thought she meant at night, but she clarified she was suggesting a morning call, which would be 8:00 AM California time. It seems that my mailed material arrived at the home of Greg's parents, and when passed along, both Kelly and Greg liked what I had written. One item I had included was a song, *"My Pre-Game Routine."* Greg was interested that Cal Ripken, Jr. had written to me about the song's lyrics, and Kelly said that Greg wanted me to sing the song to him. Kelly and I talked for nearly an hour, and she was perfectly delightful.

Kelly Harris was understandably enthusiastic about her husband's remarkable baseball accomplishments and insisted that he belonged in the Hall of Fame. This former runner-up to a "Miss California" title said that she and Greg had only been married for the past two years, but that many years earlier, they had been high school sweethearts. The missing years were not discussed, but Greg had married another person, and they had a number of children before that marriage ended in divorce. Kelly showed her sympathy for the first wife by saying that someone should write about the amount of stress placed on the families of many professional baseball players, especially the wives. Before ending our phone conversation, Kelly encouraged me to ask Greg about certain experiences that she knew were important to him (like his trip to Alaska to play summer ball), and she also asked me: "What's a curve ball, exactly?" I laughed at her question, and it made me appreciate how honest and open she was as a person. Greg was a lucky fellow to have found Kelly a second time.

Before calling Greg on Friday, April 10, 2009, I jotted down some of the information that had stayed with me from numerous sources. I remembered that he had been the property of nine different teams during his 15 year Major League career, and with some effort I could name them. They were the New York Mets, Cincinnati Reds, San Diego Padres, Texas Rangers, Cleveland Indians, Philadelphia Phillies, Boston Red Sox, New York Yankees, and Montreal Expos. With all of these moves, Kelly's concern about the resulting stress on Greg's first marriage was understandable. Basic stats were available on Greg's playing days, but I came up with some interesting calculations of my own, and all were to Greg's credit. The batters facing him over his fifteen years in the big leagues must have had an average of no more than .235, and Greg had recorded a strike-out for every 4-5 batters he faced. He only averaged one walk in ten batters faced, and some of those walks must have been intentional. Considering that Greg was fully capable of throwing with both arms for most of the fifteen years he played in the Majors and considering that being ambidextrous has been his apparent claim to fame, it is startling to find that of the more than 6,000 batters faced in his big league career, he threw left-handed to only two of those batters. He wore his famous glove the day he faced those two batters, the glove that he designed with four fingers and two thumbs, a glove capable of being worn on either hand.

My Friday 8:00 AM phone call was answered in California by Kelly, and she called Greg to the phone. Greg and I chatted for a while without the conversation going in any special direction, and it seemed that Greg expected to respond to a series of questions that I had prepared. Before questioning Greg, I decided to first share some of my own baseball experiences, and he seemed genuinely interested in hearing them. I mentioned that I had actually batted against an ambidextrous pitcher in a high school game in 1948, and I could not imagine any athletic feat to be more difficult in all of sports than a pitcher throwing with both arms. The idea that someone would do it at the Major League level was unthinkable, in my opinion.

In one other experience, I recalled using the smallest bat I could find against the best fast-ball pitcher in the Maryland State Baseball League. By not using my usual Rogers Hornsby style bat, my swing was quicker, allowing me to hit a home run off of Harvey McCutchin. On my next trip to the plate, Harvey evened the score by throwing his first pitch at my head. He missed my head, but the toss did break a bone in my hand and I was out for the rest of that season. Greg said that he knew two of my former baseball coaches, Jim Boyer (a former big league umpire) and Mule Haas (a former star player for the Philadelphia Athletics). Like Greg, I too had a special ball glove. Mine was a three-pronged mitt for use at first base. I bought it in 1944, the same year that I met 16 year old Nellie Fox. Nellie was a rookie at the 1944 Athletics' training camp in my home town of Frederick, MD, and his efforts to play first base for the Athletics would not be rewarded. As stated elsewhere, his first baseman's glove would never make it to the Baseball Hall of Fame, but Nellie would make the Hall as a star second baseman for the Chicago White Sox.

My first question for Greg asked how he got started pitching with both arms. Had his father or a coach suggested that he give it a try? Greg said "No!" to both questions. It was something he felt comfortable doing, and he stayed with it even though those around him generally frowned on the effort. Greg was so successful in his early years of baseball that he was offered contracts by big league teams in 1974, 1975, and 1976. He thought he was ready to play at the higher levels, but those around him talked him into rejecting all three offers. In the summer of 1976, the offers he longed for suddenly disappeared, so he journeyed to Alaska to play in a summer league especially designed for college ball players seeking recognition. Greg and his team won many awards that summer, and Greg accepted one of his end-of-summer contract offers. He signed with the New York Mets in September of 1976 and his pro career was underway.

Greg surprised me when he said that he did not throw his first curve ball until the age of seventeen. In his earlier years, he relied solely on his fast ball and his change up to have great success on the mound. Without a curve ball, there would have been little motivation for a pitcher to attempt to throw with both arms. Greg shared with me his test for judging a pitcher's readiness to pitch with the second arm. Greg's second arm was his left, and he could meet all three requirements he had established in the test: 1) pitches had to exceed 80 miles per hour in velocity; 2) pitch selections had to include an effective curve ball; and

3) out of 35 pitches thrown to the plate, at least 30 had to be in the strike zone. I responded by saying to Greg that many big league pitchers today could not meet the third requirement even with their number one arm.

I wanted to hear more about his unique pitcher's glove. Greg said he designed it, and he had a recognized company produce it. He said he still had a number of the gloves safely stored in his home at the time of our phone conversation. The glove he designed had four fingers and a thumb on each end, allowing the glove to be worn on either hand. During team practices, he often ran and caught flies in the outfield, and during these times he said he wore the glove on his right hand, throwing with his left arm. Greg never mentioned throwing batting practice left-handed, but if his coaches saw him doing it, they would most likely have stopped the action at once. Greg said his glove violated no Major League rules, and he in fact used such a glove in his history-making 1995 game against the Cincinnati Reds.

I knew there would be humor connected to his description of the time he hurt his elbow throwing sunflower seeds into the stands from the dugout. I asked: "Is it true that you actually hurt your elbow in this way?" "Yes!" was his quick response. I said that his coaches would naturally be upset with what some might call rather juvenile behavior, but even his father no doubt expressed displeasure with him. Greg's said his father said nothing about the incident but rather sent him a package. "What was in the package?" I asked. Greg replied that his father had sent him a slingshot to use for future sunflower tosses into the stands.

Greg's longest stay with a team had been his five

seasons with the Boston Red Sox. He played for them in the 1990, 1991, 1992, 1993 and 1994. The next highest number of seasons spent with a team was 1985, 1986, and 1987, the years spent with the Texas Rangers. At Boston, the coaches were pleased with Greg's right-handed throwing, but never gave his left arm any serious consideration. I had heard that Greg sometimes worn his special glove to show his displeasure with the coaches decisions. When asked about it, Greg would not admit that any friction existed between himself and the coaches. Days after my phone conversation with Greg, I came across a picture of Greg in a Boston Red Sox uniform, and he was on the mound throwing with his left arm while wearing his special glove. If not intended to irritate the team coaches and management, why else would such a picture have been taken? Perhaps the photo proves that Greg had a great sense of humor, because during his entire five seasons with Boston, Greg had never thrown a single pitch to a batter with his left arm. Also, it appears he signed the card *Cy Harris*, perhaps comparing himself to the immortal baseball pitcher, Cy Young.

Greg was willing to describe the inning in which his life-long dream was finally realized. His Montreal team worked it out that he would be allowed to use both arms in pitching one of the final games of the 1995 season. He expected to enter that game earlier, but his appearance was limited to Cincinnati's last inning at bat. After a brief warm up of his right arm (he was not allowed to warm up both arms), he faced Reggie Sanders and got the right-handed hitter to ground out to the shortstop. Next came two left-handed hitters, Hal Morris and Ed Trubensee. Greg turned his back to home plate, and returning to the mound, his glove was now on his right hand. The batter and the umpire had to have been shocked to see Greg prepare to throw left-handed. Having had no warm up tosses with the left arm, Greg was wild and threw one pitch all the way to the backstop. He walked Hal before getting Ed to ground out. Since the next batter was right-handed hitter Bret Boone, Greg again switched the glove, this time to his left hand, and he retired the final batter on another weak infield roller back to the mound. The game ended and Greg had accomplished something never before done in the modern era of Major League baseball, pitching with both arms in a big league ball game. Greg's dream was finally realized.

Did Greg's achievement bring him the attention that it seemed to merit? Perhaps not! Greg reasoned that his playing for Montreal was the cause of the lack of interest in the event. Had he been pitching for a team in this country rather than a team in Canada, the news media may have given the event more coverage. The most noteworthy phone call to his home the next day was from the baseball Hall of Fame. This call, requesting something like a signed game ball for the museum, came as no surprise to Greg. He was happy to honor their request, but he suggested that he give them a different item to commemorate his unique accomplishment. The Hall of Fame welcomed Greg's gift suggestion, which was his pitcher's glove with four fingers and two thumbs.

Greg's impact on Major League baseball has required rules committees to focus greater attention on the rules governing switch-hitters and switch-pitchers. Just what is an ambidextrous pitcher allowed to do and not do? How often should a switch-batter be allowed to position himself on different sides of home plate? Greg said that current rules require a pitcher to stay with the same arm used on his first pitch to a batter, and a switch-hitter can change sides of the plate only until he has received a count of two strikes. I mentioned that there seems to be some debate about a switch-pitcher facing a switch-batter, and the question is: Who must first indicate his intensions? The batter wants the pitcher to indicate which arm he will use, and the pitcher wants to know the batter's position at the plate. It was Greg's opinion that rules generally are aimed to protect and favor the hitters rather than the pitchers, and if Greg is correct, this suggests that baseball fans prefer to see high scoring games rather than see pitchers throw no-hitters.

Greg retired from big league play after the 1995 season, and as any movie script would have it, his life-long dream was realized just prior to the close of that last season. Greg continues to contribute to the sport of baseball by coaching college-age players, and perhaps his love for switch-pitching and switch-hitting will rub off on some of them. The life of Kelly and Greg Harris is worthy of a movie in my opinion, and while they are both still young at heart and young in appearance, I feel that they should be allowed to play the lead roles in the film. I'd be willing to be an extra in such a film. If the movie's director allowed that to happen, I'd like to be seated in the stands next to Greg's dad, and we could catch sunflower seeds that might be thrown our way from the dugout.

Greg Harris   **Kelly Harris**

BALTIMORE COLT TRAINING CAMP MEMORIES

In June of 1958, I returned to my alma mater as an employee of Western Maryland College. Six years had passed since my graduation, and during those years I had completed two years of graduate study at Wesleyan University in Connecticut, two years of required military service at Ft. Monmouth, NJ, and two years of teaching in the Math Department of Madison High School in Madison, NJ. At WMC, I was to open the first Admissions Office in Western Maryland's hundred year history. For an undisclosed period of time, I would reside in the Albert Norman Ward Hall, a dormitory for male students, and meals were to be available in the College's dining hall.

To my pleasant surprise, the players for the Baltimore Colts professional football team were arriving on the Western Maryland campus at exactly the same time, and their training camp would apparently run for six to seven weeks, until early August. The Colt veterans and rookies would be housed in the men's dormitory directly across from mine, staying in the dorm called Daniel MacLea Hall. Their special meals would be served in a separate room of the WMC dining hall, only a few steps away from their dormitory. Colt players were quoted as saying that they did not receive any special diet at these training camps, but the food served by Mr. Rice was certainly a number of grades higher than the food served to the WMC students and quantities were huge. Adjacent to our two dorms were the Gill Gymnasium and the practice football fields.

In the 1960s, no one could deny that the college in Westminster was a perfect location for the Colts, being less than one hour's drive from Baltimore, and a bit more than that from Washington, DC. On the negative side however, some of the WMC facilities were less than adequate for a professional football team. The dorm rooms for the Colts were small, as were the beds, and one would wonder how a player the size of huge Bubba Smith would fit into a dorm-size bed. Bubba, a lineman, must have exceeded 6' 7" in height, and his weight was something over 300 pounds. I believe he wore size 16 shoes. MacLea dorm had no air conditioning and no elevators, and July and August temperatures typically reached the 90 degree level in Westminster. A single phone was in each dorm hallway, and shower rooms were shared. Gill Gym lacked suitable locker space, and the College's weight-lifting equipment was almost non-existent. Nonetheless, the Colts and their fans loved the selection of Westminster as their training site in the late 1950s and early 1960s, and a growing number of Colt fans would pack picnic lunches for their visits to the beautiful 100 acre campus.

If my memory of those early Colt training camps is correct, I doubt that any weekday group of Colt fans ever numbered more than 300 or 400 people, and the only items I can remember that were available for purchase were cups of lemonade. Mr. Rice's student workers brought the beverage from the College's dining hall in new garbage cans, and the drinks were served in paper cups to thirsty Colt fans, sold at a reasonable price, of course. The College had a nine hole golf course, and the ninth fairway paralleled the Colt's main practice field. If a shot was sliced by a right-handed golfer, the ball could quite possibly land near the Colt fans or even land near the Colt players on the football practice field. I often enjoyed playing golf on the College's nine-hole course, but seldom would I play during the times of the Colt's practice sessions. My greater worry was that a Colt player would suffer a sprained ankle by tramping on a golf ball that was left there after a golfer's shot strayed from the ninth fairway.

Admissions and student financial aid duties took a large portion of my time during that summer of 1958, but I was still able to observe some Colt practices and I enjoyed my limited contact with some of the Colt players. My absence from Maryland for the prior six years was the reason that most Colt players were unknown to me, but the names of Johnny Unitas, Raymond Berry, Gino Marchetti, and Lenny Moore were ones that I knew well. Whenever I spotted Raymond Berry seated on his dorm steps, I naturally walked across the quadrangle to sit near him. He would chat a bit as he strengthened his grip, squeezing what resembled tennis balls. Out of uniform, Raymond appeared slender in his slacks and sport shirt, and his glasses made him look like a young college professor. It is legendary how he and Johnny Unitas were often the last to leave the practice field, and when Johnny was not available, Raymond had fans toss the ball to him. On a few of those occasions, I had the thrill of actually having a catch with the great Raymond Berry. I was embarrassed when I made a wild toss which required Raymond to make an acrobatic catch, but he responded that those were the types of catches that needed the most practice.

Just by chance, that Colt team of 1958 went on to win the NFL Championship, and they repeated the success in 1959. In addition to Unitas, Berry, Marchetti, and Moore, other team standouts included: Alan Ameche, Ordell Braase, Art Donovan, Jim Mutscheller, Jim Parker, and big Bubba Smith. Weeb Ewbank was the Head Coach at that time, and he gets the credit for selecting players like Unitas and Berry in the mid-1950s football drafts. It is reported that Berry was not selected until the 20th round of the draft, and Raymond claims he arrived at Colt training camp in his first year with little knowledge about being a pass receiver.

In 1959, I was fortunate to meet a Westminster girl that I would marry in June of 1960. The girl was Carol Jennette, a former Miss Maryland and the daughter of Dr. Carl Jennette. It was also fortunate that Dr. Jennette happened to be the Colt's doctor during their training sessions in Westminster, MD. My father-in-law's close association with the Colt players and coaches naturally increased my opportunities to meet players and to attend Colt functions. Wife Carol and I always had tickets to attend Colt home games, thanks to her father, and our seats were always in the upper deck of Memorial Stadium and on the 50 yard line.

After the birth of our son, Bill, numerous photos were taken with Colt players. On the left, Billy Ray Smith lifts Bill high. As I look at these photos, some four decades after they were taken, I am reminded that the 1961 Colt fans did not seem to linger around the campus after the camp sessions ended. Unitas, Smith, and Orr, as pictured in the photos, are still seen in their practice uniforms, but visiting Colt fans are totally absent from campus scenes.

Four decades later, fans would not have left the campus until all players escaped into the privacy of locker room areas. Hall of Fame star Johnny Unitas is shown as he smiles for the camera, and Jimmy Orr poses with Dr. Jennette and Carol, and Bill.

These photos taken in 1961 serve as vivid reminders to me that 1961 was the year that Billy Ray Smith and Jimmy Orr first joined the Baltimore Colts, and both players quickly proved their value to the team.

I have no way of truly comparing the Colt training camps of the early 1960s to those of other professional teams, but I am of the opinion that the Colt camps were on a par with those camps. Also, self-motivated players like Berry and Unitas gained far greater benefits from the camps than did most other team players. Unitas and Berry were usually the last to leave the practice field. Dr. Jennette was generally found in the Colt training room nursing the bumps and bruises of players, especially the pains of those younger players attempting to catch the eye of certain coaches. On occasion, a

player or two would come to Dr. Jennette seeking to be excused from a practice session, and those giving a lame argument were shown a four-inch needle. Dr. J said that the appearance of the needle seemed to cure most of these ailments, and once it even cured Lenny Moore.

My memoir on the training camps of the "old Baltimore Colts" in the late 1950s and early 1960s is being written 52 years after my exposure to the camp of 1958 held on the Western Maryland College campus in Westminster, Maryland. To our regret, Johnny Unitas is no longer with us, and Billy Ray Smith passed away at the age of 66, but both are still vivid in our fond memories of the early Baltimore Colts. In recent weeks, my efforts to speak to one of the Colt players of that 1958 training camp was rewarded, and I was thrilled when the voice on the other end of the phone said: "Yes, this is Raymond Berry."

Raymond had just returned from one of his numerous trips, and he was about to tackle his vast amount of mail. His current web pages promote his video on the fundamentals of pass receiving, and Raymond continues to be popular on the speaking circuit. Being the true sports idol that he is, Raymond did not cut me off, but rather said this was not a bad time to talk. He shared more than a half-hour with me over the phone, and both of us enjoyed the time to reflect on the "Unitas to Berry" football era.

Raymond's dedication to his craft is legendary, and he insists that his knowledge about pass catching was minimal when he joined the Colts. He thanks Weeb Ewbank for giving him the chance to play with Unitas and Moore, two of the greatest athletes in pro football history, and Raymond pledged total effort on his part in developing the required skills for success. By his second year, Raymond's skills were perfected, and he and Unitas were thinking as one.

Raymond's video on pass receiving is a testimony to his belief that "Practice makes perfect!" By doing the required work on drills and pass routes, Raymond came to the point of perfection, and this guaranteed his success as a player and later as a coach. I knew that he believed his greatest football catches were three that he caught late in the 1958 Championship Game against New York, but I mentioned that I viewed his number of fumbles while a professional to be the most incredible of all his statistics. We did not discuss it, but claims are made that he only had one fumble throughout his 13 years of professional play. Jimmy Orr, the other great end for the Colts, played about the same number of years, and he had a total of 8 fumbles in his career.

Before Raymond and I concluded our phone conversation, I touched upon some topics other than football. My wife mentioned that he had accepted an invitation to speak to the Westminster Methodist Church congregation one Sunday morning in the 1960s, but Raymond could not recall the event. Some Colt teammates claimed that they cleaned up their language a bit when in Raymond's presence, because of his religious nature, but I was never aware of such a modification in their behavior. Raymond laughed when I told him that Billie Ray Smith, Jr., often visited our Westminster home, and at times he rested his feet on our living room coffee table, while still wearing football cleats. At that time in the 1960s, his father, the Colt lineman, owned a Westminster home quite close to our wooded property. My son, Bill, maintained a friendship with Billie Ray, Jr., and visited with him in San Diego, CA, while he gained fame as one of the greatest Charger players. Billie Ray, Jr., was truly a "chip off of the old block," as he followed in his father's footsteps.

I asked Raymond about his 1958 appearance on the TV program *"What's My Line."* I had not seen the actual program, but I assumed that the panel had not guessed Raymond to be a professional football player, especially if he wore his glasses that evening. Raymond explained that the Colts had just lost a Sunday game in New York, partly due to the fact that Johnny Unitas was injured the prior week, and the backup quarterback had to play. After losing in the final few minutes of the game, a Colt official asked Raymond to appear on the New York based "What's My Line" program, and he naturally accepted the assignment. A week after my phone conversation with Raymond, I actually viewed the video tape of that 1958 *"What's My Line"* program, and it was not what I expected. Moderator John Daley tried to hamper the panelists, but Dorothy Kilgallen quickly narrowed Raymond's occupation to entertainment and sports, and Bennett Cerf then locked in on the Sunday football game and mentioned that Raymond made a catch that nearly won the game for the

Colts. Later in the broadcast, Bennett Cerf mispronounced the name of the great Johnny Unitas, and the kidding Bennett received was justified.

In March of 2010, Raymond wrote to me saying: "Thanks for the memoir writing you sent. A lot of great memories got stirred! Those were special days with special people – the team, the fans, the City/State. We were all fortunate to be a part of it . . . over 40 years later we are still enjoying the memories!" Raymond also sent the photo shown below which includes four Hall of Famers. In the photo from left to right are: Raymond Berry, Weeb Ewbank, Lenny Moore, and Johnny Unitas. All four were major contributors to the success of the Baltimore Colts in the early years.

RECREATION AND HOBBIES, OTHER THAN SPORTS

This category is a catch-all type of category, and I touch only on music, Sudoku games, and memoir writing. You and other readers of my material could think of many other topics that could be included under this heading. My brother once collected stamps, but I never got that bug. My parents enjoyed playing cards, especially a game called "Five Hundred." In graduate school, I did enjoy a card game called "Oh Hell!" A great feature of that game was that any number of players could join in. Another interesting feature of "Oh Hell" was that you had to make your bid exactly, taking the actual number of tricks you bid, no more and no less. In other words, if you bid three tricks and took six tricks, three points were then deducted from your score.

Rob Reynolds, my son-in-law, likes to collect old cars, and some people are hooked on antiques. Maybe you are a bird watcher or fly your own private plane. Regardless of your interest, there are others who share that interest, perhaps forming a club. The key to a happy life is to stay active.

SINGING AND COMPOSING MUSIC

Singing has been a part of my life since about the age of four. At that age, I began singing duets with my brother, Charlie, who was six at the time. We were a popular attraction in the Frederick, MD, community, and all invitations to sing were accepted. Our father drove us to the event and our mother was the accompanist. Mother played the piano for Trinity Methodist Church Sunday School and she played the organ for church services. Dad sometimes joined in the singing, but most of our family singing took place around the piano in our home. Throughout my entire life I was a member of church choirs and community choruses, and for most of that time, I was the tenor soloist for the various groups. There was never a fear of appearing on stage and performing in public, and tenor soloists were always in demand wherever I went.

When I attended the Charlotte Hall School for one year, I was the soloist for a dance band, and after that, I entered college in Westminster, Maryland. There, I not only sang in choirs and choruses, but I also had three years of voice training and took classes in dramatic art. This was my first exposure to acting in plays and musicals. Next came my two years at Wesleyan University in Middletown, Connecticut, and I sang in the Wesleyan College Choir and the Middletown Methodist Church choir. Since Wesleyan was an all-male school at that time, we often joined with the great all-female Radcliffe College Choir for concerts. Then came the two years spent in Madison, New Jersey, singing in the local Methodist Church Choir as tenor soloist. During that two-year period, the Centenary College in Hackettstown asked me to fill roles in their campus musicals. For my two year military service obligation, I was stationed at Fort Monmouth, New Jersey, and while there, I sang in all of the musicals and choir programs of the local Red Bank Methodist Church. On the military base, we formed a barbershop quartet which competed in the All-

Army Talent Show, and we just missed appearing on the Ed Sullivan Show. My next change of residence returned me to Westminster, Maryland, and numerous musical experiences, and some of those are pictured below. In one photo, I perform the JB Biggley role in "How To Succeed . . . ," and in another, I play the Admiral role in "H.M.S. Pinafore." My role as the Padre in "Man of La Manche" and my part as Sid in "The Pajama Game" were other enjoyable stage experiences.

I became Governor of Rotary District 7620 in 1997, and this was the point of my entry into composing music rather than being strictly a singer of music. My first song written for Rotary clubs to sing was "Secure Rotary's Tomorrow by Securing Youth Today," and my Rotary International President for that year was Glen Kinross of Australia. The message he left on my Westminster answering machine was at first viewed as a possible prank by some local Rotarian, but to my surprise, Glen received my return call at his Chicago apartment. He asked me to sing my music over the phone, and he actually gave it some consideration as his International Theme Song. My song was not selected, but Glen and I became the best of friends, and for years, we joked about his poor judgment in selecting a theme song in 1997 other than my own. One of my later songs, titled "What All Rotarians Know," called upon the use of some twenty themes adopted by past-presidents of Rotary International. Almost every living past-president wrote to me about that song, expressing their pleasure at seeing their themes as part of the song's lyrics.

BJ's Treasure Girl

The Admiral and Miss Buttercup

My collection of Rotary music expanded to 36 pages in length, and the Google search engine picked up portions of the collection from various Rotary web pages, especially the Rotary Zones 31-32 web pages. Since the year 2000 or 2001, the collection titled *"Songs for Rotarians"* has appeared under such Google listings as *Songs for Rotarians, Rotary Songs*, and *Rotary Singing*. The category *Rotary Songs* often includes more than a million items, and my *"Songs For Rotarians"* is usually placed at the top of page one. I am often asked the reasons for the collection retaining its top rating on the Google and Yahoo lists, and I can only guess at the answer. The numerous quotations of past-presidents of Rotary International certainly has an impact, but the bigger reason, in my opinion, is the fact that no other entry actually provides music and lyrics that can be downloaded by Rotarians around the world. It must receive many hits to stay on top of Google's lists.

"My Pre-game Routine" is one of the songs in the Rotary songbook, and the lyrics could stand alone as a memoir of my experiences coaching and playing sports. The words are best suited to the sport of baseball, and a former baseball super-star sent me his response to the lyrics. That super-star is none other than Cal Ripken, Jr. The lyrics fit Cal perfectly, because of his dedication to daily routines and because his father was his coach.

[Typical pre-game announcements go: Please allow the players to play, the coaches to coach, and the officials to officiate. Failure on the part of any fan to cooperate will lead to an immediate ejection from the premises.]

MY PRE-GAME ROUTINE

1. Some "so-called sports fans" never meet a real star,
   content to watch T. V. placed over a bar.
   I go to the park to get into the fray,
   no lesser involvement would brighten my day.
2. Before my big game I require eight hours sleep,
   rule out restless turning and counting of sheep.
   I get up well rested, my breakfast is light,
   and when we're victorious, I'll have my next bite.
3. I first do my chores, that is no "Hocus Pocus,"
   cause once the game starts,
   all good players must focus.
   My shoes, they've been shined, and my uniform's
   clean, rosin bag in my pocket, my senses are keen!
4. I do vocal scales, want the voice to be strong,
   to call out to teammates, tell umpires they're
   wrong.
   My Gator Aid's packed, and my muscles are
   limber,
   I'm eager to bat and grab hold of that timber.
5. All that I have said could have led you astray.
   My son is the one who is pitching today.
   I'd like to be playing, but say it I daren't.
   You should hear the truth now, I'm only a parent!

August 9, 2006

Dr. Kenneth Shook
301 Stoner Avenue
Westminster, MD 21157

Dear Ken,

I hope this letter finds you well. I just wanted to take a moment to thank you for sending me the song My Pre-Game Routine. I always enjoy taking a look back at my career and remembering all the pre-game rituals.

Thank you very much for your support throughout my career. Without fans like you, my baseball career would not have been such a huge success. It is very rewarding today to be able to give back to my fans.

Thanks again!

Sincerely,

Cal Ripken, Jr.

A Cal Ripken, Jr., response in 2006

ADDICTION TO SUDOKU PUZZLES

Prior to being introduced to Sudoku puzzles, I was a person who enjoyed all types of logic problems. One story I enjoy sharing took place in my senior year of college, and when my date for the senior prom took ill, she arranged a date for me. I would rather have remained by my date's bedside, but she insisted that I attend the dance. The girl she selected for me was very pleasant, and she apparently did her homework. Whenever the band took a break, she was prepared to fill the void with logic problems. Her supply of logic problems seemed to be endless. She helped me to enjoy the evening, overcoming my earlier disappointment.

Most persons cannot usually identify the one individual who introduced them to Sudoku puzzles, but for me, it happened to be my much older brother (by two years). Charlie, who is a Methodist minister, surely sent me the puzzle with all good intensions, and he tempted me with money if I was able to solve the Sudoku challenge. He knew that I had no prior exposure to such puzzles, and the "DIABOLICAL" rating on the puzzle meant nothing to me. As any younger brother must, I accepted his challenge. Within several days he received the completed puzzle, but this Methodist minister withheld his payment until I wrote a three-page strategy for solving Sudoku puzzles. After that, my fame grew, and my knowledge of Sudoku spread far and wide. I began conducting Sudoku sessions in the local libraries of my home community, Carroll County, Maryland, and one of those first sessions had twelve persons in attendance. The librarian said that an event was judged to be successful if at least three participants attended, and all were surprised when the local newspaper sent a photographer to cover the Sudoku workshop story.

If you wondered why these people, ranging in age from ten to as old as 39+, gave up their evenings to discuss this new number game, I wondered the same thing. One answer seemed to be that the puzzle was new, and it was reported to be the fastest growing and most popular game puzzle in the world. It went to New Zealand and Australia, and finally Sudoku emerged in the United States in 2005. My home newspaper began publishing Sudoku puzzles in early 2006, and that was when I accepted the call to conduct sessions on the new Sudoku craze.

The puzzle is fun for most people, and solutions require no math calculations. One woman in a Sudoku session insisted on adding the digits, so I corrected her behavior by substituting nine letters for the puzzle's nine numbers, the letter a replaced 1, b replaced 2, etc. During that evening session, we solved the puzzle using nine letters, and then we returned to puzzles that use only the digits 1-9. I have heard it said that Sudoku is relaxing and beneficial to one's mental health, but I have also heard of cases in which family members race for the morning paper, thus claiming ownership of the single Sudoku puzzle printed there. I suppose that these dysfunctional families could subscribe to more newspapers, or, they could regain family happiness by seeking free puzzles off of the Internet.

After four or five years of Sudoku sessions, I concluded that the instruction of new players was no longer required in Carroll County. I suppose that everyone could have mastered my strategy for solving Sudoku at that point, but somehow, I find that logic a bit hard to accept.

CONDUCTING MEMOIR WORKSHOPS

It was in 2005 that I conducted my first workshops at local libraries and at local book fairs, and those sessions focused on one of two topics, namely *How to Solve Sudoku Puzzles* or *Writing & Sharing Memoirs.* My brother had sent me a Sudoku puzzle from Florida and promised $5.00 if I could solve it. The puzzle was foreign to me, but the thought of getting money out of my brother was a challenge I could not resist, so I sent him my solution within 24 hours. He responded with an additional requirement before I could claim the reward. He insisted on a detailed explanation of how the puzzle was solved. My three page explanation must have met his demands, because he sent the $5.00 and I framed it. Had it been a check, I would not have framed it. Word circulated in my local community that I had developed a logic for solving Sudoku puzzles, and I agreed to conduct workshops on the new number game.

My love for writing and sharing memoirs had its start several years before 2005, thanks to a request made by my oldest son, Bill. He asked me for a special Christmas gift, unlike gifts given in past years. He wanted some old photographs, placed in an album of some sort, and we would make it an annual practice to discuss the pictures at Christmas time. I can recall that the first album was such a hit that hours passed before there was any thought of opening the other gifts. Interest in discussing the photos and sharing stories of the past motivated me to begin writing my personal memoirs with greater frequency, and these so called "snapshots of life" soon reached seventy to eighty in number. As was the case with Sudoku puzzles,

I wanted to share my love for memoirs with others, and workshops on memoirs were scheduled starting in 2005.

Expanding on the comments I made on page xi, agenda questions to be answered at workshops are: 1) What is a *memoir*? How does writing a memoir differ from keeping a personal diary or doing a school research paper on a particular topic? Could memoirs be recorded rather than written? Does a written memoir have any desired length? Could a memoir include photographs and sketches? Could it be a poem and not a short story? 2) What events in a person's life are worthy to be included in one's memoirs? Does a memoir event or topic have to be a "once-in-a-lifetime" happening, and something that few other human beings had ever experienced? Could the memoir experience possibly be something that many people have experienced? Could it be a current topic, rather than something that occurred many years in the past? How are topics selected? Could a magazine or an old photograph act as a trigger for generating memoir topics? Are any topics or personal experiences off-limits for public airing and unsuitable for presentations? Who has veto rights? 3) What audience or group of readers does the writer of memoirs have in mind? Is the writer writing only for family members (children and grandchildren), or is the finished material intended to be shared with a broader audience? 4) Are there "ground rules" which a writer of memoirs should follow? Must all statements in a memoir be true? Will your memory ever fail you? Could the experiences of others ever be included in your recorded memoir? 5) Does writing memoirs about unpleasant experiences ever have a therapeutic impact on the writer? Should writing memoirs always make the writer feel good? 6) Once written, what should happen to memoirs? How should they be preserved? How should they be shared?

A panel was selected to join me on some of these workshops, and each panelist was asked to share an experience or happening that could become a memoir. Jean Worthley, who had appeared on a popular TV program, *Hodge Podge Lodge*, shared her experiences as she taught children to enjoy the marvels of nature. Panelist Doris Pierce said she could think of nothing to share, and then she related a gem of a life experience which I use to conclude this memoir. Her happening is titled: *Santa & Mrs. Claus Visit St Louis*.

My workshops revealed to me that most people do not know what memoirs are, and once they do, they find that the task of writing one's memoirs is fun and workable. Many in each audience left the room highly motivated to begin collecting a list of possible topics for memoirs, and they seemed determined to write or record on tape some of their most memorable life experiences. They realized that such precious moments could easily be lost forever, unless an effort is made to prevent such an outcome. Doris Pierce's story is an excellent example of one life experience that is worthy of becoming a memoir. Hopefully she will recall others.

Sam & Doris Pierce at work

Doris Pierce speaking:

Sam and I often bring joy to children and their parents by assuming the roles of Santa and Mrs. Claus. The attached photo was taken at a meeting of the Westminster Rotary Club in December of 2006. Sam is the force behind this Christmas activity, and he actually allows his beard to grow several months before the Christmas season to prove to children that his beard is not fake. One December, Sam suggested that we dress as Santa and Mrs. C and fly to our daughter's home in St. Louis for a surprise visit. When I got through coughing, I realized that he was serious about the venture. In a moment of weakness, I agreed to don the Christmas costume, and airline tickets were purchased, from Baltimore to St. Louis, with a brief stop in Atlanta.

We were met at the BWI airport by a red cap worker, but he quickly decided that his services were needed elsewhere. Our mode of dress and our luggage in bags rather than in suitcases must have given him second thoughts about our mental state. I also had some doubts about our mental state. Children and dogs followed us through the terminal, and it was a relief to board the flight to Atlanta. I wanted to hide in my seat, but the pilot naturally mentioned our presence on the plane, and all passengers strained to have a look at the distinguished guests. If we were listed as guests, why did we have to pay for our tickets? The Atlanta airport was also an experience, as Sam got a big hug from some un-named blonde. She wanted to know what he had for her in his sack of goodies. Do you think she did not recognize me as Mrs. Clause?

The flight from Atlanta to St. Louis was eventful also. As before, the pilot welcomed our presence on the flight, and our every need was met by the hostess in our section of the plane. A small boy came from the rear section to gaze at Sam, I mean Santa, and the boy asked: "Santa, why are you flying?" Quick thinking Santa replied that his sled had a broken runner, and we were having it repaired in St. Louis. The boy thought about the answer for a moment, and then he said "Okay" and returned to his seat. We were the last to leave the plane in St. Louis, thank heavens, and our daughter nearly collapsed when she saw us enter the terminal. Her hands went to her face as she gasped "Oh, no!" . . . . Looking back, I now believe that Sam's idea for a surprise visit met with success, but one such experience was enough for this Mrs. Claus.

EVENTS THAT DEFY LOGIC AND BEAT THE ODDS

When you have an experience in life which approaches the unbelievable and no logical explanation is at hand, it would seem to merit inclusion in your group of memoirs. Some people hearing such a remarkable tale become discouraged and conclude that they have no happenings in life worthy of preserving or sharing. For this reason, I have sometimes hesitated a bit when I'm asked to share my "white-light-experience" at memoir workshops. Regardless of the consequences, if you hit the lottery, you must surely want to share the good news. On the other hand, how do you cope with bad-news happenings? If your event was a negative in your life, do not rush to judgment. Some decide not to relive a bad dream, while other find great benefit in finding friends who will listen with sympathetic ears.

My three memoirs in this category have no disturbing elements, and the first two could cause you to shake your head in disbelief. Enjoy!

MY POPE PIUS XII PHOTOGRAPH SESSION

On my first major tour of countries outside of the United States, I visited England and numerous countries on the European continent in 1957. Other than a single trip into Canada, I had never been outside of the USA, and I had never had a flight in a plane. Perhaps my most memorable experience while on that tour of Europe was my photograph session with Pope Pius XII in the Vatican in May of 1957.

From early childhood, my family had always been Methodist, but my interest in singing religious music caused me to offer my services to many churches that were not Methodist. For many years, I was the choir soloist for my own Methodist church as well as the local Christian Science church, singing at each church every Sunday morning. Being a Methodist did nothing to lessen my expectation that my 1957 visit to the Vatican would be one of the highlights of my European tour, and this proved to be the case. In May of 1957, I arrived in Rome, nearing the end of my 46-day tour. The first sight that I visited was the Coliseum, which at one time was the entertainment center for ancient Rome where gladiators and lions engaged in mortal combat. That was followed by my visit to the Pantheon (the temple to "all the gods"), the Spanish Steps, and the Trevi Fountain. I recall tossing a number of liras into the fountain for good luck. Last but not least, my attention was directed toward the Vatican.

As I stood in St. Peter's Square and looked at the Basilica, which dated back to 1614, I wondered if my "Trevi Fountain luck" would cause the Pope to make an appearance at his window high above the Square. True, he would have been several hundred yards away from me, but none-the-less, it would have allowed me to claim that I actually saw the Pope on my 1957 visit to Rome. Well, it was not to be, since he made no window appearance, but I later had a photograph session with Pope Pius XII. My explanation of this event with the Pope though true resembles the experiences of a fictional character such as Forrest Gump. After spending hours seeing the glories of the Sistine Chapel, I was passing through a very large room of the Vatican, and attendants suddenly rushed in and began using ropes to form a wide aisle. I moved forward and pressed my legs against the ropes, hoping that some noteworthy event was to take place shortly. Whatever the event, I would be positioned in the first row.

The room that had been nearly empty of visitors quickly filled to capacity. The crowd seemed to sense that some dignitary would appear, perhaps even Pope Pius XII. Shortly thereafter, four strong men entered through the door at the far side of the room carrying Pope Pius XII, seated in his elevated chair. The chair resembled a throne, and the Pope was regal in appearance, wearing the glasses usually seen in his photographs. He was perhaps a bit smaller than I would have expected, but he commanded everyone's attention. He wanted to be close to his subjects, and they wanted his touch and his blessing. The Pope was leaning far to his left side, attempting to reach the hands extended upward toward him, and I was positioned on that left side.

I had no doubt that the Pope was always welcomed enthusiastically by Catholics wherever he went, but on this occasion, he had an excited Methodist in his midst. This spiritual moment caused a surge in my emotions, as it must have for a woman standing some twenty rows behind me. This person was perhaps Catholic, because she did not hesitate to begin passing her baby over the heads of those in front of her, hoping the Pope would bless her baby as he passed by. The hands of at least twenty persons were needed to move the baby forward to the path followed by the Pope's procession. The baby suddenly came over my right shoulder and landed in my arms. Here I was with a baby I had never seen, and here came the Pope approaching me down the aisle. The Pope's attendants and his personal photographer were leading the procession.

An attendant came to my assistance, and the two of us held the baby high for the Pope to bless. The Pope's photographer apparently decided that this was a good photo opportunity, and he captured on film the Pope blessing the child. After the procession had passed my location, the photographer approached me, and he recorded my name and address. He promised that the picture just taken would be mailed to me. Within a matter of weeks, an envelope arrived from the Vatican containing the 8 x 11 inch black and white photograph. The baby was clearly the center of attention for the photographer's shot, but my profile was visible, and the photograph would remain as one of my most prized possessions. I did not see the Pope from St. Peter's Square that day in 1957, but I could prove that his photographer took our picture on that memorable day.

In closing this episode, I remind the reader that all of my memoirs are true. If you find it difficult to believe my account of the photograph session with the Pope, imagine how difficult it is for my wife to accept my explanation of the baby in the 1957 photograph. My wife and I first met in 1959, and we were married in 1960.

MARI, THE POPE'S PHOTOGRAPHER IN 2002

One evening in the year 2002, while watching television in my Westminster home, I chanced upon a documentary showing a day in the life of the "Pope's Photographer." The man snapping pictures was identified as Arturo Mari, and I hastily jotted down the name. I noted how the Pope's busy schedule in 2002 kept this energetic photographer on the run, and the photographer was often with the Pope from early morning until late at night. As I watched his typical day unfold, I naturally reflected on my experience in the Vatican in 1957, and I even began to imagine that this man resembled the photographer who took my picture in 1957. Questions were flying through my mind. *Could this be the same photographer that took my photograph?* and, *Why, after all of these years, would this man remind me of that 1957 photographer?* The answers to my questions were provided as the 2002 TV program came to a close.

The public television program announcements at the end of the program stunned me, because the announcer revealed that Arturo Mari was completing 45 years of service as the Pope's photographer. A quick subtraction of 45 from 2002 indicated that 1957 was his initial year of service, and that he was indeed the person that had taken my picture with Pope Pius XII in the Vatican. Perhaps my next action was risky, but I decided to mail the original 1957 photograph, with identifying stickers on the back, to the Vatican, hoping for some type of response. The envelope was addressed to "The Pope's Photographer," and I also enclosed a copy of my original memoir. Many of my friends said that the photographer would never see the material due to the massive amount of mail received by the Vatican. Their criticism of my poor judgment seemed to be valid, but then a response arrived from the Vatican.

The response I received from the Vatican was in the form of a large white envelope which returned the original photograph and nothing else. No letter or note was attached, and it was possible that Arturo had not actually read my letter or seen the 1957 picture. Weeks later, I reopened the envelope, and a closer look at the photograph revealed the photographer's signature near the bottom of the picture. Arturo's signature verified that he had in fact seen the picture, and he provided the proof that it was indeed his photograph, a picture that he had taken 45 years earlier in his first year as the "Pope's Photographer." I now knew that he had retained my letter and the memoir written about my 1957 visit to the Vatican. Now you know "The rest of the story!"

* * August, 2002 Letter Sent To The Vatican * *

To: Arturo Mari, Pope's Photographer
Vatican City, Rome, Italy

Dear Sir:

At seventy-two years of age, I enjoy writing my memoirs and attaching photographs when available and when appropriate to the story. Enclosed is one of those interesting and humorous episodes. I believe that you may be part of that experience on May 19, 1957. The enclosed two pages and photograph tell the story. Several months ago, I was watching a public television station and the program placed great emphasis on the life of the Pope's Photographer in 2002. I was amazed to see that you resembled the Vatican photographer as I remembered him in 1957. Imagine my surprise when the speaker said that you were in your 45th year as the Pope's Photographer, and it appears that you came on the scene in 1957. Were you the one who snapped the enclosed photo and kindly mailed it to me? If yes, I would appreciate you autographing it before returning it to me in the self-addressed envelope.

I hope that you have fun reading my account of the 1957 incident and looking at what could have been one of your early photographs of Pope Pius XII. I also hope that you are the same person I met on my 1957 visit to the Vatican. In the 1957 picture, I am the well-hidden blonde directly behind the child, handing the girl in the white dress to the attendant. Thank you for considering my request. I look forward to your response.

Very sincerely, H. Kenneth Shook 301 Stoner Avenue, Westminster, MD USA 21157

* * * *

ZIO FOTOGRAFICO

'OSSERVATORE ROMANO

20 CITTA' DEL VATICANO

06 698 84797 - Fax 06 698 84998
E-mail: photo@ossrom.va

3,20

CITTA' DEL VATICANO
R 229582

DR. H. KENNETH SHOOK
301 STONER AVE
WESTMINSTER, MD 21157
U.S.A.

'E - PRINTED MATTER

IEGARE - DO NOT BEND

Official Vatican return envelope

208

Arturo Mari's photo, 1957 original unsigned

Arturo Mari's photo signed in 2002, 45 years later

MY WHITE LIGHT EXPERIENCE IN YEAR 2000

The year was 2000, and my annual plans to attend the Rotary International Convention each June were cancelled. Rather than travel to South America to join my Rotary friends, this year I would have both knees replaced on the same morning. Dr. Blue would perform the operation in the Carroll County General Hospital located in Westminster, Maryland, my home town. At first, Dr. Blue wanted to replace only the right knee, but an x-ray revealed that the left knee deserved equal treatment. When I told the doctor that I could not even walk the dog and that something had to be done, he knew that I was ready for the knees to be replaced. Had I asked if such an operation should be performed, his answer would have been: "No!" I had spoken to friends about knee replacements, and I liked the idea of both knees healing at the same time. Why should the process be spread out over two operations when it could be done in one operation?

The first night following the June 5th operation was my only painful experience, and that discomfort was apparently due to a malfunction of the machine that supplied the pain-killer solution. When I awoke the next morning, I was surprised to find that my knees were being exercised while lying on my back in bed. I was pedaling a bike device. Swelling did not occur in my legs, and there was relatively no pain. Having both knees replaced in one operation required that I choose a location for rehab, either Baltimore or York. My choice was the facility in York, Pennsylvania. That is where I was transported four days later.

I found the workers at the York Rehab Center to be very

dedicated people, and all went well until the night of June 15th. On that late Thursday evening, I was uncomfortable in my bed, so I eased myself into a wheelchair and positioned the chair in the lobby, near to the nurse's station. It was about eleven PM when a massive pain struck my abdomen. It felt as though an arrow had been shot through me, twisting as it penetrated my body. I was briefly reminded of childhood movies in which Robin Hood fires a twisting arrow into a target. I knew that I was passing out, so I called to the nurse: "You've got an emergency here!" My eyes must have rolled back into my head, and I did fall to the floor, unconscious. Thankfully, the Head Nurse recognized that time was critical, and in a matter of minutes, she had me in an ambulance, racing across town to the York Hospital. I recovered consciousness in the ambulance and asked: "How far to the hospital?" Someone answered: "Two minutes away!" The pain was beyond anything ever experienced in my lifetime, but I said aloud: "I think I can make that," and I passed out.

When I came to, the surgeon in the York Hospital was asking if I could sign a paper allowing the Trauma Team to operate, and I was willing to sign anything. My mind had silly thoughts, asking myself if the pen would write in the upside-down position. While lying on my back, I recall the surgeon saying that they would do their best, but that my chances were not good. Again, I passed out. While preparing me for the operation, my family was contacted by phone and notified to come to York at once, and my survival was questionable at best. My wife, at home in Westminster, MD, responded that they had the wrong party, since I was only in York for rehabilitation of my knees, and she went back to bed. My daughter did race to York, praying for me as she drove from Kutztown, Pennsylvania. At some point late in the operation, I had my white light experience.

My white light experience was dissimilar to regaining consciousness in that I felt I was somewhat detached from my body. I could not move any part of my body, and only my mind and my senses seemed to be functioning. I was aware of brilliant white light filtering through fog, telling me to not open my eyes, but there was no light at the end of a tunnel, and the light was not coming from a single source, like a light bulb. I realized that an operation had taken place, but I was not an observer. I desperately wanted to know the outcome of the operation. There was no feeling of pain or panic at this point. I asked myself if I had survived the operation. I felt very calm, and yet, I felt a bit of frustration when the female voices that I heard did not provide an answer to my survival question. It seemed that I could hear sounds from hundreds of miles away, and I felt that my mind had never been more alert and energized than at that very moment. The duration of my white light experience is unknown to me, perhaps lasting seconds or minutes, but it ended when I sensed that the brilliant light was no longer present. I then opened my eyes to find the surgeon standing next to me in the recovery room.

The surgeon assured me that I had indeed survived the operation, and he wanted me to know how fortunate I was to have lived through the experience. He pointed out that I had been hit by four aneurysms, all on the aorta, and three had been treated. He decided to pass on the forth aneurysm because I was too near death to continue. He said the typical aneurysm he repairs is about 2 cm in size, the width of the little fingernail, but that my largest aneurysm had been 10 cm in size. My odds of survival had been less than 5%. At this point, the surgeon said: "Somebody up there had to be watching out for you!" His words caused me to gulp, and they convinced me that I had truly undergone a "white light experience." I had not returned from death, but I had actually reached its threshold.

Several other doctors visited my hospital room days later, and looking at me, they said that my experience was better than any prepared script. They said that the Head Nurse saved my life by her prompt actions at rehab, and that I would have died had I been in bed when hit by the aneurysms. Had I been on a golf course when hit, I would have died. They said the entire Trauma Team had been there when I arrived, late at night, at the York Hospital, and that never happens. They were shaking their heads in disbelief as they departed my room. In record time, the surgeon concluded I was ready to be returned to rehab, but rehab had given up my bed, thinking I would never return. The Hospital was forced to keep me one additional night while rehab found a bed for me.

I was told that my surgeon was Dr. Heard, and that because of crowded medical schools, he had to go out of the country to receive his medical training. Fortunate for me, he returned to the York area to do his practice, and he was the one who saved my life. He then added to the already unbelievable episode by saying that I played tennis with his dad, Jessie Heard, of Hampstead, Maryland. Dr. Heard actually grew up in the community that is just 15 minutes from my Westminster home. As many in this memoir had said, you couldn't write a script . . . .

In the months and years following my "white light experience" of year 2000, I have shared my memoir with hundreds of people, and from that group, only two persons have claimed to have had a white light type of experience. One was a woman who could not talk about the event, because it was too emotional a time for her. The other person was a Copenhagen doctor in Denmark. His near-death experience was the result of a heart operation which nearly took his life. He said he seldom shared his "white light" story with others, but that its impact on his life was felt every day, and he felt that he had been truly blessed.

THREE "LOST & FOUND" HAPPENINGS

The three "Lost & Found" events that occurred in year 2004 all took place within the span of only seven days, and in each case, I had found an object that I knew the owner would greatly miss if not quickly recovered. I viewed the experiences as quite unique, because I could not recall ever finding objects of such value in all of my previous 74 years. Also, I wondered if my responses to the three events would have been different had I experienced them at a much younger age. In 2004, I took immediate steps to locate the owners and to return the three objects without delay. The first item that I found was a large set of keys which someone had lost in the parking lot located adjacent to the Billingslea Medical Building in Westminster, Maryland. The second item was a wallet, and it was found in the White Marsh Mall located near Towson, Maryland. The third item, which was found later that same week, was another wallet, and it had been dropped at the intersection of Green Street and Washington Road in Westminster.

In the year 2004, a third member of the Shook household was our yellow lab named Jessie. Jessie had trained me to take daily walks, and frequently we walked the grounds of the Carroll County Hospital complex. The Hospital and parking lots were located directly across the street from our Westminster home. On one of our late-afternoon strolls, the setting sun reflected off of a shinny object on the edge of the parking lot, and it turned out to be a large set of keys. Someone had apparently dropped the keys while getting in or out of a car, and now the parking lot was empty of traffic. One office was still open in the nearby Billingslea Medical Building, and the office receptionist knew of a man who had lost a set of keys. She did not know his name, but she felt certain that he would return the next day. I gave her the keys, along with my name and address. She agreed to deliver the keys to the man, stating that he had been in a state of panic over the loss, saying that the keys would be difficult to replace. I know that the keys were returned to the frantic owner, but he never contacted me with a word of thanks.

Several days later, I was shopping at the White Marsh Shopping Mall, and a wallet appeared before me on the parking lot of the IKEA Store. Cards in the wallet identified the owner to be a female student of Loyola College, and the contents included photos, credit cards, a driver's license, and perhaps as much as $60 in cash. There seemed to be no logical place to turn in the item at the Mall, so I drove to a State Police Station that I knew to be located further west on the Baltimore beltway. The policeman on duty recorded my name and address, and I suggested to him that someone contact the student as soon as possible. Delays would only add to the student's concern. Another trooper overheard our conversation, and he agreed to drop the wallet off at Loyola College that very evening. Days later, a potted plant with balloons attached arrived at my door in Westminster, and the Loyola student had added a note of thanks. Her exact words were: "I didn't know that people like you existed! Many thanks!" My heart was warmed by her response.

The third item found that week was another wallet, and this time I spotted it on the street at the intersection of Green Street and Washington Road in Westminster. I stopped the car to retrieve it, and its owner turned out to be a girl who lived about a half-mile away on the Old Baltimore Pike. The wallet contained some money, and her driver's license provided her Westminster address. It took only five minutes for me to drive to the girl's house, and it must have been her father who came to the door. I identified myself, and after hearing my story, he grunted his displeasure with his daughter's dumbness. He grabbed the wallet from my hand, and closed the door with a bang. No words of thanks were ever expressed by the father or daughter.

Having read the above paragraphs, you will understand why I rejected the title "Finders Keepers, Losers Weepers!" and chose instead the title "Lost & Found" for this memoir. During my entire lifetime, I do not recall losing any material possessions of great wealth, and seldom have I found valuable items that others have lost. It is a pleasant experience for me to return a lost item to the rightful owner, and I expect that the "Finders Keepers" mentality evaporates with our transition from youth to adulthood. That being said, wallets and keys can always be replaced, but how can the loss of a loved one ever be replaced? I have been a church soloist all of my life, and a favorite solo of mine has been "The Penitent" by Beardsley Van de Water. The lyrics that I have sung hundreds of times tell us of a son who lost his way and later finds himself and returns to his father. The lyrics also tell us of a joyous father who welcomes home a son that had been lost. In my opinion, the lyrics of "The Penitent" provide a perfect close to my memoir on the topic of LOST & FOUND.

"THE PENITENT" (St. Luke XV, 11-25) By Van de Water

A certain man had two sons; And the younger of them said to his father; "Give me the goods that falleth to me." And he divided to them his living. And the younger son gathered together, and journeyed to a far off country, and wasted his substance in riotous living. And when he had spent all, there arose a famine in that land, and he began to be in want, and no man gave unto him. But when he came to himself, he said, "How many hired servants of my father's have bread enough, and to spare, while I perish with hunger! with hunger! I will arise, I will arise, and go unto my father, and will say unto him: Father, I have sinned, sinned against heaven, and in thy sight, Father, I have sinned and am no more worthy to be called thy son. Father! Father, I have sinned, make me as one of thy hired servants, make me as one of thy hired servants!" And he arose and came to his father, who saw him and had compassion, and ran, and said; "Bring forth the best robe and put it on him, and shoes on his feet! Bring forth the best robe and put it on him, and a ring on his hand! For this my son was dead, but is alive again! He was lost, and is found! He was lost, and is found! My son was lost, but he is found!"

Dr. Ken Shook, pictured with Shadow, wants everyone to write their memoirs. He has been sharing his love for memoirs with others for many years, conducting workshops and lecturing to groups in the Maryland area. His annual appearances at the Random House Bookfair which is held in Westminster, Maryland, are well received. Dr. Shook has two memoir collections, *GETTING HOOKED ON MEMOIRS* and *WRITE YOUR MEMOIRS BY THINKING SMALL*. He has also edited two memoir collections, one for The 1952 Graduating Class of Western Maryland College and another for The 1958 Graduates of Madison High School (NJ). Numerous education articles have been printed in the *Journal of the National Association of College Admissions Counselors (NACAC)* and *The College Board Review*, and his collection of Rotary Songs has been at the top of Google search lists for many years. His book on solving Sudoku puzzles has yet to be published.

In addition to being a classroom teacher of Mathematics and Sociology, Dr. Shook was a college dean of admissions for 18 years, Executive Director of the Maryland State Scholarship Board for 10 years, served as President of the Potomac & Chesapeake Chapter of NACAC (the first male recipient of the Apperson Award), was nominated for national president of NACAC, and in 1985, he served as President of the National Association of State Scholarship & Grant Programs. Ken and Carol Shook have lived in Westminster, Maryland, for more than five decades.